S0-AEC-532

BUILDERS
OF THE
SOCIAL ORDER

BUILDERS
OF THE
SOCIAL ORDER

By
The Reverend Joseph F. Thorning
Ph.D., Litt.D.

PROFESSOR OF SOCIOLOGY
MT. ST. MARY'S COLLEGE
EMMITSBURG, MARYLAND

AND MEMBER OF THE
EXECUTIVE COUNCIL ON CULTURAL
RELATIONS WITH IBERO-AMERICA

Essay Index Reprint Series

BOOKS FOR LIBRARIES PRESS
FREEPORT, NEW YORK

Copyright, 1943, by Society of the Divine Savior

Reprinted 1968 by arrangement

261.83
T 39 b
65490
April 1969

Nihil Obstat

E. A. CERNY, S.S., D.D.
Censor Librorum

Imprimatur

✠MICHAEL J. CURLEY, D.D.
Archbishop of Baltimore and Washington

LIBRARY OF CONGRESS CATALOG CARD NUMBER:
68-57340

Dedication

To the

Rector of St. Patrick's Church, Miami Beach,

The Rt. Rev. Monsignor William Barry

An apostle of modern Florida,

This volume, as a token of admiration and esteem,

is dedicated by the author.

PREFACE

SOCIAL reconstruction is not merely a matter of principles, however spiritual and excellent these latter may be. The rebuilding of society has to be undertaken in the world of reality.

Since social justice is not automatic in its application, it is a virtue that must be realized in definite social and economic institutions. These latter have "a local habitation and a name."

The nations and the leaders, who have endeavored with varying degrees of success to actualize the Papal program of moral and economic reform, are living, breathing entities. They are engaged upon a task which calls for our sympathetic interest and attention. Some elements may be transferable to our own social economy.

To study the impact of principles upon persons and peoples has been the purpose of this book entitled *Builders of the Social Order*. As followers of Christ we are interested especially in Catholic leaders as well as in movements which have had some measure of Catholic leadership.

In advocating social justice, however, we do not overlook the beauty and the obligation of practising supernatural charity. It has been said that "there is no substitute for the good neighbor." It may be added that there has been devised no satisfactory vicar for the "Good Samaritan." Our hospitals, orphanages, asylums, sanatoria, clinics, dispensaries, social centers, schools and churches are and will remain the focal points of Catholic social life. With them we can be sure of the sanctity and learning of our leaders in the future. From them will radiate the beneficent influence of Christ's love for mankind. The way of salvation is indicated by the age-old wisdom of the Church and the Vicar of Christ.

In *Builders of the Social Order* it is evident that the author, a priest of my Archdioceses, has tried to present more than mere theoretical or academic knowledge. The emphasis is upon facts: facts, supernaturalized, to be sure, by right living and right intentions. Fortunately, there is a minimum of political or secular comment. The author wishes to see all things restored in Christ. Dr. Thorning knows that "the peace of Christ in the reign of Christ" can be achieved in the nation and in the world, *Deo volente et adjuvante.* "Where sin abounded, Grace can more abound."

The treatment is clear, succinct, direct. The principles are drawn from the *Rerum Novarum* of Leo XIII, the *Quadragesimo Anno* of Pius XI, and the *Summi Pontificatus* of His Holiness, Pius XII, now gloriously reigning. I bespeak for *Builders of the Social Order* the attention and good will of all who wish to further the Christian way of life.

✠ MICHAEL J. CURLEY, D.D.
Archbishop of Baltimore and Washington

The Feast of Our Saviour's Resurrection
April 13, 1941

AUTHOR'S INTRODUCTION

THE PURPOSE of this volume is to suggest practicable, democratic solutions to our social problems in the light of the Papal Encyclicals: the *Rerum Novarum* of Leo XIII; the *Quadragesimo Anno* of Pius XI; and the *Summi Pontificatus* of Pius XII.

In the first place, I wish to record my sense of grateful appreciation to His Excellency, the Most Reverend Michael J. Curley, D.D., Archbishop of Baltimore and Washington. This brave prelate, on every occasion, has proved a far-sighted champion of the Papal principles of social reconstruction. In Baltimore and Washington, Schools of Catholic Action have served as centers of instruction for workers, educators, professional men and women, artists, farmers and employers. Under Archbishop Curley's direction, numerous other nuclei for the dissemination of sound Christian social doctrine have been established. Best of all, the Archdioceses have given a lead in every project instinct with supernatural charity. Justice, truth and love have gone hand in hand.

Among those at Mount St. Mary's Seminary and College, who have been most encouraging and helpful in the preparation of this volume, are the following:

The Rev. Dr. John F. Cogan, dean of the College
The Rev. Dr. Joseph J. McAndrew, Spiritual Director of the Seminary
The Rev. John J. O'Neill, professor of Modern Languages
The Rev. Peter A. Coad, professor of History

The Rev. Dr. Elwood S. Berry, professor of Dogma

The Rev. James G. Burke, professor of Greek

The Rev. Hugh J. Phillips, Librarian and Archivist

The Rev. Joseph P. O'Donnell, professor of Scripture

The Rev. Dr. John A. Weidinger, associate professor of philosophy

Dr. John J. Dillon, professor of English

Dr. Wilfred Garvin, professor of Economics

Mr. Kenneth Jackson, professor of History

Mr. Frank Moritz, professor of Education

Some of the material in this book appeared originally in The Catholic World, The Sign, Columbia, the National Catholic Welfare Conference News Service, The Washington Post, The New York Times, Light (organ of the International Catholic Truth Society), America, The Commonweal, the Religious News Service of the National Conference of Christians and Jews, The Field Afar (organ of the Maryknoll Foreign Mission Society of America), The Catholic Review (official publication of the Archdioceses of Baltimore and Washington), The Florida Catholic, and The New Review (Calcutta, India). Consequently, permission was sought and received to use this material, with credit, to the Very Rev. James M. Gillis, editor of the Catholic World; the Rev. Theophane Maguire, editor, and the Rev. Dr. Ralph Gorman, associate editor of The Sign; Mr. Frank Hall, Director of the National Catholic Welfare Conference News Service; Dr. Felix Morley, editor of The Washington Post (now President of Haverford College); Mr. Edwin L. James, Managing editor of the New York Times; the Rev. Dr. Edward Lodge Curran, President of the International Catholic Truth Society; the Rev. F. X. Talbot, editor of America; Mr. Philip Burnham, editor of The Commonweal; Mr. Reginald T. Kennedy, an officer of the National Conference of Christians and Jews; The Very Rev. John J. Considine, editor of The Field Afar; Dr. Vincent de Paul Fitzpatrick, Managing editor of The Catholic Review; Mr. Charles A. Dunn, Managing editor of The Florida Catholic, and the Board of Editors of The New Review.

Credit is also to be given to the Bruce Publishing Company for permission to quote several passages of "Francisco

Franco" by Joaquin Arrarás and translated by J. Manuel Espinosa, Ph.D.

A number of valuable suggestions were made by the following friends and advisers: Mother M. Gerald, Honorary President of Barry College, Miami Shores, Florida; Mother Grace Dammann, R.S.C.J., President of Manhattanville College of the Sacred Heart, New York City; Mother M. Generosa, Provincial Superior of the Franciscan Sisters of Glen Riddle, Pennsylvania; Mother M. Marcella, President of Marywood College, Scranton, Pennsylvania; Mother Jane Frances, President of the Georgetown Visitation College, Washington, D.C.; and Mother Eleanor O'Byrne, dean, Manhattanville College of the Sacred Heart.

Among those who read the manuscript and supplied important information are the following: The Rt. Rev. Msgr. Joseph M. Nelligan, Chancellor of the Archdioceses of Baltimore and Washington; the Rt. Rev. Msgr. Harry A. Quinn, Rector of the Cathedral; the Rt. Rev. Louis C. Vaeth, Director of the Propagation of the Faith; the Rt. Rev. Msgr. John L. Sheridan, President of Mount St. Mary's College, Emmitsburg, Maryland; Rev. Brother Peter, President, St. Stanislaus College, Bay St. Louis, Mississippi; the Rt. Rev. Msgr. Michael J. Splaine; the Rt. Rev. Msgr. John M. Hegarty, Vicar-General of the Diocese of San Diego; the Rev. Cosmas Shaughnessy, General Editor of The Catholic Literary Guild; the Rev. Dr. Peter A. Reilly, of St. Patrick's Church, Miami Beach, Florida; Dr. Fred G. Holloway, President of Western Maryland College; the Rev. Dr. John J. McInerny, Regent of the Medical School, Creighton University; and the Rev. George G. Kearney of the Archdiocese of Chicago.

Acknowledgments are likewise due to the Hon. Sumner Welles, U.S. Under Secretary of State; the Hon. Leo T. Crowley, chairman of the Federal Deposit Insurance Corporation; Dr. Richard J. Purcell, head of the Department of History at the Catholic University of America; Mr. August Neumann, President of the Catholic Literary Guild; Mr. James J. Murray, chairman of the Board of Directors of the Great Lakes Dredge and Dock Company; Mr. John G. Thompson, Attorney-at-Law, Miami, Florida; the Hon. George S. Messersmith, U.S. Ambassador to Cuba; Mr. Walter Donnelly, Commercial Attaché at the U.S. Embassy; the Hon. Robert F. Wagner, U.S. Senator from New York;

the Hon. David I. Walsh, U.S. Senator from Massachusetts; the Hon. Millard E. Tydings, U.S. Senator from Maryland; the Hon. George L. Radcliffe, U.S. Senator from Maryland; the Hon. Henry Cabot Lodge, Jr., U.S. Senator from Massachusetts; the Hon. Scott Lucas, U.S. Senator from Illinois; the Hon. James M. Mead, U.S. Senator from New York; the Hon. Albert J. Engel, U.S. Representative from Michigan; the Hon. James A. Shanley, U.S. Representative from Connecticut; the Hon. Herman Kopplemann, U.S. Representative from Connecticut; the Hon. John W. McCormack, U.S. Representative from Massachusetts; the Hon. Hatton W. Sumners, U.S. Representative from Texas; the Hon. Arthur D. Healey, U.S. Representative from Massachusetts; the Hon. John P. Higgins, Chief Justice of the Superior Court of the Commonwealth of Massachusetts; Dr. Patrick F. Scanlon, Managing Editor of The Tablet; the Rev. Brother Peter, President of St. Stanislaus College, Bay St. Louis, Mississippi; Dr. John C. Hayes, associate professor of Law, Loyola University, Chicago, Illinois; Mr. Neil MacNeil, assistant Managing editor of The New York Times; Dr. George Yanitelli of Fordham University; the Rev. John J. Kehoe of Georgetown University, Washington, D.C.; the Rev. Dr. George Warth, Regent of the Medical School, Loyola University, Chicago; Colonel Manuel de la Sierra, Air Attaché of the Spanish Embassy; the Hon. Herbert R. O'Conor, Governor of Maryland; the Hon. William C. Walsh, Attorney General of Maryland; the Rev. William A. Connell and the Rev. Cyril P. Donohue of Marquette University, Milwaukee, Wisconsin; Mr. Paul May of Washington, D.C.; Mr. Paul J. Taggart of Wilmington, Delaware; Mr. Frank Hirt, Associate Professor of History at Western Maryland College; the Rev. William A. Carroll of Miami Beach, Florida; Mr. Walter Vaughan of Brooklyn, New York; Dr. James F. Lyons of Jackson Memorial Hospital, Miami, Florida; Dr. Isaiah H. Bowman, President of Johns Hopkins University, Baltimore; Mr. George M. Widney of Mobile, Alabama; the Very Rev. Percy A. Roy, President of Loyola University, New Orleans, Louisiana; the Very Rev. Florence D. Sullivan, Rector of the Gesu, Miami, Florida; the Rev. Dr. George Barry Ford, Rector of Corpus Christi Church and Counsellor of Catholic Students at Columbia University, New York City; Dr. George N. Shuster, President of Hunter College in the City of New York; Dr. Robert Wilberforce, Director, the British Library of Information, New York City; the Rev. Joseph R. McLaughlin, Rector, Our Lady Queen of Martyrs, Forest Hills, Long Island; the Rev. Dr. Gerard F. Yates of Georgetown University; the Very Rev. Edward C. Phillips of Woodstock College, Woodstock, Maryland; the Very Rev. Robert S. Lloyd, Director of Manresa Retreat House, Manresa-on-the-Severn; the Rev. Theophane Maguire, editor of The Sign; Mr. Arthur Hays Sulzberger, publisher of The New York Times; the Hon. John J. Costello, U.S. Representative from California; Dr. William P. Schoen, Jr., of the Loyola University School of Dentistry, Chicago; Mr. Eugene F. Karst of Montreal and St. Louis, Missouri; Mr. Thomas A. O'Neil of Miami Beach, Florida; Dr. Lewis C. Cassidy of the National University School of Law faculty; the Rev. Dr. Ignatius Kelly of De Sales College, Toledo, Ohio; the Rev. Dr. Joachim Bauer of St. Mary-of-the-Springs College, Columbus, Ohio; the Rev. Dr. William M. Slavin, Director of the Catholic Forum, Troy, New York; the Rev. Harold C. Hanley, Pastor of St. Gregory's Church, Brooklyn, New York; the Rev. John S. Boylan, Pastor of St. Joan of Arc Church, Brooklyn, New York; the Rev. Dr. Charles A. Meehan, Rector of St. Mary's Church, Maple Grove, Illinois; the Hon. James E. Murray, U.S. Senator from Montana; Captain John Vincent Hinkel of the U.S. War Department; the Rev. Dr. Joseph G. Gschwend, Master of Novices, St. Stanislaus Seminary, Florissant, Missouri; the Very Rev. Peter A. Brooks, Provincial, St. Louis, Missouri; the Rev. Dr. William J. McGucken, Director, School of Education; and the Very Rev. Harry A. Crimmins, President of St. Louis University.

For any mistakes of commission or omission, the undersigned alone is responsible.

JOSEPH F. THORNING, Ph.D., Litt.D.

Chairman, Department of Social Sciences
Mount St. Mary's College, Emmitsburg, Maryland.

March 25, 1941
Feast of the Annunciation of the Blessed Virgin Mary

CONTENTS

XIV

CONTENTS

XV

CHAPTER I

J. H. JEFFERSON CAFFERY

America's Ace Ambassador

"A cardinal requisite of any foreign service
diplomat is that he shall be able to write clearly,
vividly, movingly."
—TIME, DEC. 11, '39

JEFFERSON CAFFERY, United States Ambassador to
Brazil, is a son of the deep South. Born in Lafayette,
Louisiana, December 1, 1886, he grew up on his father's
sugar plantations, broad acres, rich in every form of agricultural wealth. The farm had forests, lakes and marches.
As a boy, Jefferson Caffery explored every nook and
corner of the ancestral estates on foot and horseback.
Walking and riding are two recreations he has carried
with him into adult life. Sport in the open air and under
the sun developed his muscular frame, stripping the
torso of every ounce of superfluous flesh. Trim as an
athlete, young Caffery rode to school, jousted with his
fellow students in bouts of wrestling and boxing, spent
the week-ends on the neighboring estates of friends
where fox-hunting and grand balls attracted the flower
of Southern gentry. He was graduated from this
environment a full-fledged lover of nature and an adept
in the arts of social diversion.

1

Politically as well as genealogically, Jefferson Caffery stemmed from Andrew Jackson and Thomas Jefferson. The members of his family, however, had not been active in politics. Religiously, his mother and father were members of the Episcopalian communion. The Anglican rector was a frequent house-guest at the Caffery estate. This clergyman was a polished gentleman who knew how to move in cultured surroundings. His sermons, regrettably, were long enough to induce somnolence in young and old alike. Under these circumstances church attendance for those in the Caffery household was more of a social obligation than an office of religion. There were Catholic neighbors in the vicinity, but their faith never came to the attention of the youngsters in the Caffery family. Louisiana's tradition of tolerance did not foster the animosities which smouldered in other Southern States. Catholics in the Lafayette region were regarded with good-natured forbearance by their Protestant friends. The most vivid impression the youthful Caffery gained of Catholicism was that imparted by a family acquaintance, the Hon. Joseph E. Ransdell, U.S. Senator from Louisiana.

Scholastic Background

At Tulane University, where Jefferson Caffery made his undergraduate studies, decided emphasis was placed upon American history and international law. The stripling from Lafayette showed a taste for both these specialties. In his free time he played tennis and handball. Occasionally, he varied this sports fare with a fencing match. Intercollegiate competition attracted him little. Although neither at the top nor bottom of his class, he was forming habits of careful reading and writing that were to stamp his conversational and epistolary style. When admitted to the Louisiana bar in 1909, he was known as a student rather than as an orator or special pleader.

During the next two years, he devoted every spare moment to his research in diplomatic history and admiralty law. Arriving in Washington, D.C., in the middle of 1911, he passed the examinations, written and oral, for the diplomatic service, with flying colors. His first appointment was to the American Legation in Caracas, Venezuela. It was a perfect observation post for the study of South American dictatorship. Caffery, instead of dawdling away his time at the American Club, settled down to learn Spanish. The language became his key to an understanding of the Spanish American temperament. When he left Caracas in June, 1913, he was esteemed by Venezuelan business men and politicians as a good neighbor.

FIELD OF DIPLOMACY

After a brief assignment as Secretary of the U.S. Legation in Stockholm, Sweden, Jefferson Caffery was treated to a diplomatic baptism of fire as *chargé d'affaires* for German and Turkish interests in Persia (now Iran); by a swift turnover in the military situation in the Near East, he was entrusted with supervision of British and Italian affairs in the same country.

At the conclusion of the World War, Mr. Caffery had one of his most interesting and valuable experiences. The Secretary of State, Robert Lansing, assigned him to handle details of protocol for President Woodrow Wilson in the Paris of 1919. Coming into daily contact with personalities like Clemenceau, Lloyd George,

Orlando and Col. Edward House, Jefferson Caffery came to know the confidences and the idiosyncrasies of all. One of his colleagues at this epoch remarked: "It is a matter of record that Caffery can practise reticence in twelve different languages. He is still discreet about what happened at Paris after the armistice. Wilson communicated his impressions of European diplomacy. Caffery stored them up for future reference."

It was at this period that the Louisiana diplomat began to frequent the Church of Our Lady of Victory in Paris. Of course, he was familiar with the Cathedral of *Notre Dame* and the *Madeleine*. But he loved little, out-of-the-way chapels, where he could note the swift, tense drama of the Mass. Not yet a Catholic, nor even deeply interested in the Church's creed, Mr. Caffery was studying the credentials of Christianity, investigating what we call the "preambles of Faith."

RELIGIOUS STIRRINGS

Oddly enough, scholars from three secular universities played an important part in this stage of Jefferson Caffery's spiritual Odyssey. The New Humanism, as expounded by Paul Elmer More of Princeton, Paul Shorey of Chicago and Irving Babbitt of Harvard, exercised a powerful attraction upon his inquiring mind. Devouring every atom of evidence on the authenticity and genuinity of the New Testament, Mr. Caffery decided that Scripture was sound, true, inspired. Enamored of the person of the Risen Christ, he spent hours meditating upon His words and works. Every excavation or discovery in the Holy Land elicited new interest and fervor. The American diplomat invested a generous share of his income in critical archeological studies published by American and European universities. He began to study Greek and Aramaic, because these languages held the key to an intimate knowledge of the Word of God. In order to glean a better, more scientific understanding of the Old Testament, he subscribed for the *Revue Biblique*. At every step of this progress in self-education his studies were supplemented by prayer. Most of all, he relied upon his new-found friendship with Christ.

Patrology was the next sphere of inquiry. St. Basil, St. Gregory of Nazianzen, St. Athanasius, St. Augustine and St. Ambrose were the authors of predilection for Jefferson Caffery. His own statement on this point is illuminating:

"Before I embraced the Catholic faith I made it a matter of conscience to peruse all of the Greek Fathers. Why? Because I wanted to know what took place at Ephesus and Chalcedon. These Councils were decisive in their judgments on the nature and personality of our Saviour. I remember how eager I was to grasp the full meaning of THEOTOKOS as applied to the Virgin Mary by the Council of Ephesus. I found my answer in the Latin word DEIPARA, God-bearer. And, of course, anyone who reads the Patristic authorities will go on to try to master the *Summa Theologica* and *Summa Contra Gentiles* of St. Thomas Aquinas."

LOVE OF NEIGHBOR

Engrossed though he was with things Divine, Jefferson Caffery did not fail in his love for his fellow men. One of the brightest chapters in his career is that which deals with his humanitarian activities. In 1922, he cooperated with the Greek Government and the American Red

Cross in assisting Greek refugees from Asia Minor. He also served on a large number of commissions for the help of War Cripples and was chairman of the American Red Cross Earthquake Relief Activities in Japan from 1923 to 1924. In rare intervals of leisure he attended the Holy Sacrifice of the Mass in Tokyo. Religion and humanitarianism went hand in hand.

Up to this point Mr. Caffery's service in the diplomatic corps was that of a subordinate official. He had ascended through the regular grades of the department, strictly upon the basis of merit. Two qualities in his character were noted by his superiors: a terse, luminous power of expression and an ability to inspire trust among foreign peoples. These gifts paved the way for Jefferson Caffery's promotion to the rank of Envoy Extraordinary and Minister Plenipotentiary to Salvador. He held this post from 1926 to 1928, perfecting his knowledge of Central America and excelling in the fluent use of the Spanish language. This assignment also afforded an excellent opportunity to continue the Scriptural and humanistic studies that were gradually leading the young diplomat into the Catholic Church.

It was at this time that Mr. Caffery made the following remark to one of his friends: "Christ and His Sacrifice are the irresistible mysteries and sublime realities of Catholicism." Simultaneously, he began to use the Missal when he assisted at the ceremonies of the Holy Mass. Almost literally, he had followed the Victim of the Altar, a clean oblation, from one continent to another, "from the rising of the sun to the going down thereof."

His studies kept pace with his devotion. The *Revue des Sciences Philosophiques et Théologiques*, edited by the Dominican Fathers of Saulchoir, Belgium, arrived regularly on his desk; the *Dublin Review* was another visitor. The Minister liked articles with depth and tone; he traced statements to their original, primary sources; weighed every assertion in relation to the findings of recognized scholars. The lowbrowism and sentimentality of certain sections of religious literature did not attract him. In fact, by their exaggeration of some purely external manifestations of devotion, a number of practices tended to be obstacles to his embracing the Faith. He could not be satisfied with superficial reasons or approximations of truth.

CONVERSION TO THE CHURCH

Speaking on this subject, after his conversion, the American statesman declared:

"Thousands outside the Catholic Church could be won to the Faith, if it were properly presented to them. Intelligent men and women realize the futility and emptiness of agnosticism, as either a philosophy of life or a practical system. They want a reasonable interpretation of their place in the universe in terms of religion, but they are, in many instances, deterred from the Catholic Church by what they think they see on the surface. They imagine certain pietistic practices are superstitious and, looking no further, they remain outside the fold. Christopher Dawson and Karl Adam are the sole authors skeptics are apt to read. Spokesmen for truth, well versed in the arts and sciences, are needed to make a synthesis between religion and modern learning —something like what Origen did in his age for dogma and Greek philosophy. No one can read the Greek Fathers and remain unpersuaded of the truth and beauty of Christianity."

Another promotion was in order in 1928. Important negotiations were in the offing between Colombia and the United States. Caffery had proved his competence in the Spanish American field; he was chosen to act in Bogotá as Minister Plenipotentiary. But, before he assumed his duties, Mr. Caffery determined to resolve his final difficulties about revelation. In Washington, while receiving instructions from the State Department about his future role in South America, he seized the occasion to consult a prelate at the Catholic University of America about the so-called "implicit-citation" passages in Genesis. This particular prelate, who was an expert in history, referred his questioner to a priest-scholar, who had specialized in Scriptural studies. The doubts were speedily resolved and, after conditional Baptism, the happy convert was confirmed by a missionary Bishop in New York.

His gratitude for the supernatural gift of Faith was deep, sincere. The whole process was completed modestly, quietly, without fanfare of trumpets or undue publicity. A splendid gentleman and deeply patriotic American had brought his love of Christ to full cycle. He was now able to receive his Eucharistic King into his own heart, glowing with fervent joy.

LATIN AMERICAN EXPERT

For the next five years, Jefferson Caffery did a high-class job for the United States in Colombia. President Olaya Herrera of that country became a warm friend and admirer. American interests in Colombia were the beneficiaries of this relationship. Another prominent citizen of Bogotá, Archbishop Ismael Perdomo, publicly spoke of the American representative as his "best friend." For his part, Mr. Caffery liked the Colombians and found much to praise in their attitude toward God. The people of Colombia, he never tires of repeating, are both *croyant* and *pratiquant*.

In the meantime, a new Administration came into power in the United States. President Franklin D. Roosevelt and Secretary of State, Cordell B. Hull, were both aware of Caffery's qualifications. The President in particular had followed the young Louisianian's career with keen, personal interest because they had both served Woodrow Wilson in a critical period of American history. Mrs. Sarah D. Roosevelt, the President's mother, who had been in Paris in the immediate post-war epoch, knew how expert Caffery had been during the days of the Versailles conference and in the humanitarian activities on behalf of refugees from many lands. These recollections did no harm in 1933. In fact, they prompted the President to give Mr. Caffery his first Ambassadorial appointment, that to Havana, Cuba. Had State Department routine been observed, the assignment probably would have been something like that of Ambassador to Turkey. But Cuba was a hot spot in 1933 and an ace career man was required.

Before Caffery actually took up his duties in Havana, however, the post of American Ambassador there was ably handled by Sumner Welles, now Under Secretary of State. Caffery, as Assistant Secretary of State for Latin-American Affairs, spent some months in Washington acquainting himself with the broader aspects of administration and laying groundwork for the first reciprocal trade treaty of the new Administration. This was the exchange agreement with Cuba, the cornerstone of Secretary Cordell Hull's foreign policy. Acting under the direction of the President and Mr. Hull, Jefferson Caffery accomplished the grinding, daily negotiation which culminated in a mutually advantageous commerce between the United States and Cuba. Incidentally, the treaty was instrumental in improving the Cuban labor situation sufficiently to ward off the imminent threat of revolutionary Communism.

SUCCESS IN CUBA

When Jefferson Caffery reached Havana, American prestige was at a low ebb. There were frequent demonstrations against U.S. "imperialism." Marxist agitators stirred up the people against American diplomats and business men. Strikes were rampant in the public utilities and on the railways. Here and there sugar mills were burned. The workers, existing on the level of starvation, were ready for "direct action." They were encouraged and supported by the Leftist President, Dr. Ramón Grau San Martin. The latter, surrounded by a host of Marxist intellectuals, made no secret of his admiration for the methods of Moscow. The Soviet was closer to our American shores than at any other period of history.

Within a few weeks, this situation underwent a radical change for the better. Grau San Martin was ousted by his fellow Cubans. Colonel Fulgencio Batista became the actual head of the State. Order was restored to the Island. To be sure, the Batista régime was a military dictatorship, but it did not permit anarchy or a Soviet reign of terror. Improvement in the economic status of the workers, due to the treaty with the United States, allayed popular unrest. A breathing-space was provided, preliminary to an effort to restore constitutional government. American diplomacy, led by Cordell Hull and implemented by Welles and Caffery, achieved what many commentators have described as "a first-class political miracle."

The happy result was not achieved without drudgery as well as danger. Day after day, Ambassador Jefferson Caffery began the many tasks of his office by attendance at Holy Mass. His chauffeur, often threatened with death, had orders to take his chief to a different church or chapel each morning. In that way, thanks to the mercy and Providence of God, the bomb-throwers and assassins were thwarted. Not once did the American Ambassador show the slightest apprehension or fear. Fortified by the Sacraments, he went forth each morning to a *rendez-vous* with God. His confidence was justified. A bomb wrecked the Embassy garage, but no other damage was done.

SUCCESS IN BRAZIL

Once the Cuban scene had resumed a measure of tranquility, a new post was in readiness for Mr. Caffery. The President appointed his ace diplomat Envoy Extraordinary and Ambassador Plenipotentiary to the United States of Brazil. This was in July, 1937. The assignment admittedly, was to the most important diplomatic job in Latin America. It was another indication of the esteem and confidence which his record as a career diplomat had inspired in the President and Secretary of State.

Immediately upon his arrival in Rio de Janeiro, Ambassador Caffery undertook the study of Portuguese (something which his predecessors had neglected) and in a few months he was able to converse fluently in the language of the country with Brazilian leaders. As a result, President Getulio Vargas and Foreign Minister Oswaldo Aranha became his admiring friends.

In August, 1937, Brazil was in the throes of political turmoil and our trade, due to the compensation-mark system, was declining seriously. Ideologies, alien to this Hemisphere, were making bold efforts to strike root in South America. On November 10, due to a *coup d'état,* an *Estado Novo* (New State) was installed in Brazil. Ambassador Caffery, by maintaining intimate contact with Brazilian leaders, employed all his tact, patience and understanding in diverting the new régime from Nazi-Fascist channels. Brazilian policy was maintained in the broad, deep tradition of the closest political and economic cooperation with the United States. Subsequently, both President Vargas and Foreign Minister Aranha expressed to this writer their appreciation of the good offices of Mr. Caffery throughout this critical era.

An American resident of Rio de Janeiro summed up for me his impressions of the Ambassador in these words:

"Jefferson Caffery has catholic interests. He is equally at home in commerce, finance and in the domain of arts and letters. He has taken a profound interest in cultural interchange between Brazil and the United States. His support was responsible for the unusual success attained by an exhibition of American books in Rio de Janeiro. The Brazil-United States Institute, the principal cultural link between our two countries, is now a thriving concern, due largely to his interest and sympathy."

LOVING AND BELOVED

The climax of Ambassador Caffery's social career was reached in his marriage, with Sebastian Cardinal Leme presiding, to Miss Gertrude McCarthy of Chicago. This charming lady was the daughter of a high-ranking Army officer, Brigadier-General Daniel F. McCarthy, whose organizing genius worked wonders for the military forces of this nation during the World War. The *Chatelaine* of the U.S. Embassy in Rio de Janeiro has won golden opinions from the members of the diplomatic corps in Brazil. She is worshipped by the Brazilians. "Americans are proud of the affection in which the Ambassador's wife is held by the Brazilians," remarked a prominent member of the British colony to me. "Mrs. Caffery is the most gracious hostess in Rio."

An American citizen, Mr. Theodore Xanthaky, who has lived and worked in Rio de Janeiro for twenty-five years, does not hesitate to say:

"Under Ambassador Caffery's sure guidance, relations between Brazil and the United States are measurably better today than they have ever been. He is certainly the most respected and, at the same time, the most popular diplomat accredited to Brazil. His dignity and charm, coupled with the fact that both he and his spouse are Catholic, have completely captivated the Brazilian people. At the same time, it is the concensus of opinion among American businessmen in Rio de Janeiro that no American Ambassador in recent years has done so much for the development of trade between Brazil and the United States."

The Ambassador, be it added, is still an athlete. He can compete with his friends in tennis and swimming, now his two favorite sports. An indefatigable worker, he occasionally takes time off to climb the principal mountain peaks in Brazil. He is a first-class alpinist and recently scaled the *Dedo de Deus* (Finger of God), a particularly hazardous feat. The Brazilian press devoted many columns and pictures to his courage in this accomplishment. His love of Christ continues to be expressed in assistance at Holy Mass and reception of the Blessed Eucharist, on six of the seven mornings of the week. On Saturdays, with commendable common sense, he takes a "late sleep." It is a respite from labor and duty that is well deserved.

The career men in the Department of State are happy about the achievements of Jefferson Caffery. In their eyes, he is an example of the fact that promotion by "the hard way" is possible. Able diplomatist and great-hearted humanitarian, he richly merits the title of AMERICA'S ACE AMBASSADOR.

CHAPTER II

EAMON DeVALERA

Eire Explained

WHILE THE bombs fall on Europe, Africa and the British Isles, the most Christian nation in the world is trying to maintain a precarious neutrality, or if you will, non-belligerency. The emphasis in Eire is not upon mass production of warships, pursuit ships and artillery, but upon efforts to secure a "more abundant life" for the workers in factories and on farms. Furthermore, sincere, scientific consideration is being accorded to the problems of the so-called white-collar workers. The tone and temper of this program of reconstruction is reflected in the words of a statesman, who, for all the discussion his policies have evoked, must be considered to have held the center of the world's stage for a longer period than any of his contemporaries.

This exclusive interview, which took place in the Hon. Eamon DeValera's private office in Leinster House, may have the merit of presenting an image of what the whole world ought to be, according to the mind of the Holy See and the best Christian statesmanship, after a tragically destructive war. Cooperation, not conflict, is the keynote of these conversations. The whole picture offers to the democratic nations some hope of a brighter

15

future for the common people: the real soldiers of society.

Asked about the economic and financial background of social reform, the Premier replied:

"Under our native government we have greatly expanded our tillage area. For example, today we are able to produce practically all our sugar, due to intensive cultivation of the sugar-beet and the construction of huge refineries. Formerly, we were dependent upon imports. More than one-third of the grain that is used for bread grows on our own soil. And the national diet has been improved by a larger domestic consumption of beef, butter, eggs, chickens, cheese and other dairy produce.

"Industrially, progress has been striking. A rich variety of goods, formerly secured from abroad, is now made in our own workshops and factories. Two illustrations may be enlightening: in 1931 wearing apparel, both cotton and woolen, was imported into Eire to the value of $27,500,000. This figure has been cut five-sixths in the current year. Imports of clothing are now less than $5,000,000. Ten years ago, footwear costing the people fully $7,500,000 was brought into Eire. Today, that sum has been reduced more than ten-fold: imports of boots and shoes now amount to less than $500,000. These statistics, comparatively studied, suggest that the Irish people have achieved a fair measure of industrial independence. Economic self-sufficiency is a direct result of political freedom and in turn strengthens the fabric of our State's sovereignty.

Mr. DeValera acknowledged that more remained to be accomplished in building up heavy industry, machinery of large-scale production and insuring a steady supply of basic raw materials. These problems necessarily have been complicated by the war.

In the financial sphere the Premier pointed out that every Eire Government, since 1920, had managed to balance the budget as well as to keep the national debt within extraordinarily narrow limits. He insisted that this had been done without any impairment of the services for public health, education and housing. Indeed, as this correspondent noted, the slum clearance program in Dublin is a model for the civilized world. Only one "depressed" district remained in what was once the "slum metropolis" of the Old World.

The Irish Free State's attempt to build a Catholic state embodying the occupational group system, or vertical guilds or unions of employers and the employes in the same industry, was the next topic of conversation between this writer and Prime Minister Eamon De Valera, in the first interview he gave after relinquishing the presidency.

Based on the Encyclical of Pope Pius XI, *Reconstructing the Social Order,* Mr. DeValera asserted this "adventure into the realm of socio-economic planning will take distinctively Irish lines." He added that the state his government is attempting to devise for Ireland would be both modern and conservative.

"For the present," he declared, "it represents a philosophy, an outlook, a tendency and an attitude, suffused by principles of sound Christian teaching. The ideal of a Catholic state embodying the vocational group system will grow clearer and clearer with the practical application of the pertinent passages of the new Irish

Constitution. It will keep the compass of State from being deflected too far either to the Fascist Right, with all of its perils of state absolutism, or to the Marxist Left, with its desperate, despiritualized emphasis upon the things we eat and drink and wear.

"By frankly facing every possible objection to the twentieth century revival of the guild system, and more particularly by bridging the chasm between business and politics, we in Ireland will do our part in helping to effect the Christian social revolution."

Significantly enough, the *Taoiseach* (Gaelic for Prime Minister), as Mr. DeValera is called throughout Ireland, did not speak of corporations, syndicalism or the corporative state in telling of his government's experiment with the occupational group system. Instead he used the terms "vocational bodies" or "functional groups."

In explaining why he did this, he said that the present conflict between Communism and Fascism rendered the problem of the occupational group system, as well as its accurate exposition, a matter of acute importance.

"We know perfectly well the viciousness and lamentable results of Marxist materialism wherever it has been tried," he declared. "We are also aware of the dangers inherent in a program which would submerge individual and family liberties in blind worship of an infallible state, such as Naziism proposes. There is a reasonable, practical position which lies between the radical extremes: it consists of a modernized guild system, embracing both employers and workers in vocational bodies in every branch of industry, agriculture, commerce, the professions and the arts. This is the system we believe best fitted for Ireland.

"Obviously, these vocational groups must have the support and sanction of law. The representatives of capital and labor in each arm or instrument of production should have a voice in determining the maximum volume of output, prices, wages and profits.

"A plan of this character would put industrialists, financiers, and manual workers upon an equitable basis in the production and distribution of wealth. It would bring about effective, fruitful profit-sharing both in industry and agriculture.

"In fact it may be doubted whether any profit-sharing plan, however laudable, can operate successfully unless the employes are lifted from the level of mere wage-earners to the status of co-managers and co-directors. Since this species of partnership would not necessarily be effected upon a fifty-fifty basis, but in accordance with the enterprise, skill, zeal and capital investment of each individual engaged in the productive process, it would retain the best features of our present economy—namely, personal initiative, the opportunity for private gain, permanency of investment and security of employment."

The success of the Trades Council in Great Britain was cited by him as an indication that much more can be done along these lines. The Irish dairy industry, he said, where cooperative principles have been developed on a notable scale, would easily be among the first to benefit by the extension of this principle. Electrical workers and producers likewise could be organized with a minimum of friction, he declared.

Mr. DeValera insisted that the principal motive of the present Eire Government in attempting to develop the occupational group system, is the confidence that the Irish, as a Christian people, have in the recommendations for a better social order made by Pope Pius XI in his encyclical.

"It is inevitable," he continued, "that Ireland, with her tradition of profound religious fervor, should be in the forefront of those nations, like Portugal, Spain and Brazil, which are endeavoring to achieve a practical realization, within the limits prescribed by the national temperament and genius of each, of the Holy Father's positive remedies for the social and economic ills of the world.

"This implies that Christian ideals of the family, of public service, and of personal self-discipline and sobriety take precedence over questions of wages, prices or profits."

He frankly admitted, however, that there were two possible drawbacks to his program of social and economic reconstruction for Ireland. The first of these, he declared, was the danger of monopolistic control of a particular commodity, such as bread, by members of a certain guild or group, with consequent interference or infringement on the rights of others engaged in other spheres of production. The second possible difficulty involves a fair method of securing representatives of industry, commerce, agriculture, the professions and the arts upon a truly vocational basis, he said.

Some measure of state supervision or control would settle the first difficulty, he added. It was his view, he said, that this indispensable measure of coordination might be achieved by means of a Supreme Economic Council. This council, he explained, would be subordinate to the political organs of the state, yet vested with sufficient independent authority to keep effective control upon all factors in the process of production, distribution and consumption. Something of this kind has been attempted, it may be observed, in the establishment, at the outbreak of hostilities in Europe, of a Ministry of Supplies, which supervises and coordinates measures necessary to meet Eire's economic needs and simultaneously exercises control over prices to prevent profiteering.

"This is equivalent," the Premier commented with a smile, "to guiding a four-in-hand of spirited Irish thoroughbreds over a steeplechase course with obstacles of the number and variety of those in the Grand National —or the Irish Sweepstakes!

"Unless this was done, however, the national economy would speedily run out of focus. The prime concern of those responsible for the efficient, just administration of the vocational group set-up, therefore, is coordination and balance."

With reference to the second difficulty, he said that Ireland had had an unhappy experience with functional representation in the Irish Senate. It was the purpose of his government, he explained, to secure a representative Upper House by allowing a number of vocational bodies to nominate candidates. These candidates in turn were elected by a college composed of both *Dail Eireann* deputies and of representatives chosen by local authorities, he declared.

"As things turned out," he said, "the Senate, contrary to our expectations, tended to show a distinct political complexion, not vastly different from the *Dail Eireann* itself.

"Perhaps this is not so surprising when we recall that most of the legislation that has been considered by the most democratic assemblies any place in the world has been enacted under stress of economic deterioration. Consequently, the legislators themselves have been obliged to show a vast preoccupation with measures for public relief, social security and financial reform.

"In other words the politicians have been forced to expend the resources of statecraft upon problems that, strictly speaking, pertain to the province of sociologists, economists, bankers and health officers.

"Government today demands a degree of specialization in each one of these spheres, unparalleled in history. To draw a straight line between the realm of politics and the domain of business in the large sense of that term, is well-nigh impossible in the contemporaneous world. That is what suggests the practical advantages of the Supreme Economic Council I have mentioned, whose function would be to act as a balance-wheel between a purely political chamber and its socio-economic counterpart, the functional chamber.

"The supreme importance, therefore, of obtaining an Upper House reflecting the social and economic laminations, aspirations and needs of society, is evident. In Eire, as you probably know, one-half of the members of our Senate are elected vocationally. If the medical profession, for example, is to impinge properly upon the legislative calendar of the day, it is imperative that this occupational group be enabled to place in nomination and to secure the election of a physician or surgeon of undeniable professional qualifications, as well as of the finest Christian, ethical outlook. A horse doctor or even a competent veterinary surgeon with a flair for the turf would hardly meet these requirements."

This correspondent, who had just concluded a survey of social and economic conditions in Spain and Portugal, asked Mr. DeValera if Ireland's experiment with the vocational groups' system would follow the general lines of its development in those two countries. His answer was most emphatic.

"It would be a big mistake to imagine that Ireland, which is a small, compact, unitary state, would be induced to follow the lead of a nation whose federal or regional character is as pronounced as that of Spain or Brazil," he said. "Here we do not desire states within a state. Our history shows that Ireland prospered most when the "High King" did not find his power too jealously disputed by his brother kings in relatively powerful kingdoms. Particularism of this type would not work in Ireland. Our adventure in the realm of socio-economic planning will take distinctively Irish lines."

In conclusion, the *Taoiseach* emphasized that the unity of Ireland would comprise the finest possible contribution to social reconstruction. "The Constitution of Eire," he explained, "provides a basic law for the whole island. Sooner or later, the Northern Counties will complete the cycle of Irish independence. Economically, this will produce huge gains both for North and South. For years, there was a concentration of manufacturing industries in Ulster. The people of that region have a wider experience in trade and commercial development than those of the one-time Free State.

"Business acumen and business enterprise will stimulate every phase of our national life. These qualities abound in the North. They are a necessary complement to the traits of a people with a long tradition of success in agriculture and cattle-raising. Union of effort and commingling of talent will enrich the Irish pattern of work, study and play.

"Above all, the pooling of resources in a united Ireland would give to every Irishman a sense of confidence, pride and strength that would key the national defense program to the highest possible pitch. Since the world is contracting, due to swifter means of communication and transport, it is imperative that Eire take advantage of the opportunity to expand to her *natural frontiers*. After all, isn't that the meaning of democracy: majority rule for the commonweal?"

N.B. Acknowledgement. The author of this article wishes to record that the above interview was arranged through the courtesy and kindness of the Rt. Rev. Monsignor John M. Hegarty, Vicar General of the San Diego Diocese, a personal friend of Prime Minister Eamon DeValera.

CHAPTER III

DR. EDMUND A. WALSH

An Appreciation of Vilfredo Pareto

WHEN the four massive volumes of Vilfredo Pareto's great work, *Trattato di Sociologia Generale,* appeared in a translation by Andrew Bongiorno and Arthur Livingston, somewhat of a sensation was created. The original appeared in 1916 in Italy, and it was whispered that Mussolini had drawn much from it. There had been a great eagerness to know what was in it, but few had the courage to attempt a reading.

One of the first and, it may be added, one of the most discerning commentators on the work of Vilfredo Pareto was the Regent of the Georgetown University School of Foreign Service, Dr. Edmund A. Walsh, whose Washington lectures have for twenty years been an intellectual challenge to the élite of the Capital. For this reason, when this writer wished to secure an authoritative judgment on the scope, depth, and value of the contribution to social thinking made by the Italian economo-sociologist, it was natural to turn to a scholar who had long been familiar with the Paretan methodology.

25

The interview which resulted in this article took place on the eve of Dr. Walsh's departure for Europe and almost with the sound of the siren of the Mediterranean liner, Exachorda, ringing in his ears. And there was something of the Paretan sweep and magnificence of outlook in the title of the lecture course (complete on the desk before me) which the Georgetown savant was to deliver at the Academy of International Law at The Hague: "International Organization: The Fundamental Principles of International Life." It was another clue to the competence of the critic who was to submit his analysis of Pareto.

"In chapter one," began Father Walsh, "we discover what we had long suspected. Sociology means nothing more or less, quantitatively and qualitatively, than universal knowledge. Heretofore, we had been inclined to think that this was an attribute of God alone. Is this surprising when we remember that Pareto was by profession a railway and mining engineer, who later accepted the chair of political economy at the University of Lausanne and accumulated astonishing erudition in history, literature, philosophy, the social sciences, metaphysics, and mathematics? If, as a consequence of these four ponderous volumes, Pareto has given to the sociologists an apt definition of their science, that in itself is no small achievement. But how many sociologists can master the mountain ranges of erudition which tower above the plains of all the individual sciences?"

"In that case," this writer inquired, "just what is Pareto's contribution to social thought? How does his work constitute an advance on the Positivism of Auguste Comte?"

"It has this much in common with the method of Comte," replied Dr. Walsh, "that Pareto is concerned merely with the observation of what has happened to social relationships. It is a purely experimental sociology, using *experimental* in the sense that the physicist does, or the chemist. Pareto is only interested in what experience records. Above all, he wanted his findings to be rational and exact. He saw no reason why the social system should not be as architectonic as the solar system and as precise as astronomy. His own words on the subject are classic: 'My sole interest is the quest for social uniformities, social laws.' This is the language of the biologist in his laboratory, or the technician bending over a microscope. Are you astonished then to read that some admirers compare the *Trattato di Sociologia Generale* to the *Principia* of John Newton?

"Over and above Comte, however, the Italian sociologist, under the inspiration of his dominant idea, added mass and iteration to the positivistic method. On the physical side alone, Pareto has gathered factual information, illustrations from history and literature, events from ancient and modern times on a scale that throws Comte decidedly into the shade.

"The Frenchman did no more than sketch his sociology in rough crayon; the Italian added contour, color, background, details, and a vital principle. The skeleton not only takes on flesh and blood; it walks and talks and gesticulates. Professor Livingston is correct in declaring that Pareto embraced 'the whole complex of relations between the individual and the group to which he belongs.' Perhaps we could describe the four volumes, packed with erudition, foot-notes, and parenthetical observations, as a stupendous history of the human race in the sphere of the relations of the individual to the group, of persons, *in quantum sunt associati.*

"Where Pareto surpasses Comte, however, is in the depth of his analysis of the psychic processes in the individual. Personal reactions are then synthesized into conclusions. What an advance upon the positivistic system it is to take the figures in the Battle of Waterloo, from the common soldiers to the Duke of Wellington, place them under the magnifying glass and get one combatant's reaction. Of few scholars may it be said so truly as of Pareto that, like Leibniz, the 'windows of his cell looked out upon the universe.' He progressed measurably along the road that leads to the watch-tower where Thomas Aquinas viewed the marching panorama of humanity.

"*Par excellence,* of course, Pareto was a mathematician. This shows up on almost every page he wrote. Mathematical formulae, with all the rigidity of calculus, are liberally interspersed through the four volumes. The human objects which are the matter of his study are conceived of as mathematically perfect machines which can be automatically operated and controlled. Touch this button or that and you get a scientifically accurate result. It is as if Pareto, the engineer, throwing switches and turning valves in the control room of a great power house, pointed out the motivation and arc of conduct in these words: 'I have shown you how it happened in these persons on other occasions; you may confidently expect that it will happen again'."

"Does he then recognize cause and effect?"

"No; because that would imply philosophical thought. There is no framework of philosophy in Pareto. It is not that he despises ultimate causes; he simply ignores them. There is a wealth of fact, of description, collation, and classification. But there is no trace of values. Nor sanctions of conduct. Nor discussion of free will. Nor hint of ethics, although there is frequent mention of religion and morality."

"What place has religion in his scheme of things?" this writer ventured.

"Regrettably, he often confuses superstition with religion; more than once he identifies it with Mithraism and other scraps and remnants of paganism. Although Pareto professes the most detached attitude with respect to Christianity, Protestantism, and the world religions of the Orient, he deliberately, yet forcefully throws the whole weight of his influence in favor of a positivistic morality. Most of this leads naturally to pallitions of greed, free love, and commercial piracy. In short, where a view of human relationships is provided without reference to God or His law, the assault on organized religion, though unplanned, is for that very reason all the more subtle and dangerous. One glance at the Paretan dismissal of the 'natural law' and the 'law of nations' suffices to show the endless perspectives of moral riot and anarchy opened up for the individual and for society.

"To be sure, Pareto does not deny the fact or value of religion. But he does refuse to enter that realm. In this, he is at least consistent, because where the intrinsic essences of things are assumed to be irrelevant, there will be no concern for more than the observation of human phenomena. The sub-title of these four volumes might well be 'Intellect Only—Who Spoke of the Will?' And if you find this inadequate, you are confronted with peremptory challenge: 'If you do not agree or accept this approach, stop reading this book!' And then, to cap the climax for this champion of the mind, we find the disarming declaration: 'Just what *true* means nobody knows!' "

Recalling that Pareto has been styled the "Karl Marx of the Bourgeoisie" and that Mussolini has reputedly learned the possibilities of the totalitarian state at the knees of Pareto, this correspondent inquired whether the ideas of the master had actually been reflected in Fascist action.

The reply of the Georgetown Regent was spontaneous and clear:

"Pareto was an aristocrat of the aristocrats. He was a most deadly enemy of Marx. The metaphysical dream world of the Marxists filled him with contempt. He was not one to suffer doctrinaires gladly. He did believe in a ruling class and the necessity of others being subject to authority. That is why he is in a sense the post-humous prophet of Fascism. But altogether too much emphasis has been placed on his celebrated statement about the 'circulation of the élite.'

"Aristotle, it will be recalled, called this same phenomenon the 'cycle of degeneration.' In two paragraphs of less than a hundred words the Greek prince of the philosophers described a fact which the Italian of modern days is hard put to compass in some hundred and fifty copiously annotated pages. Every careful reader of Aristotle will recognize the discovery. As in the comparison with Comte, we must decide that the prime contribution of Pareto is another tag over the door, an accumulation of details, more case-work, more *clinical* material.

"In Pareto's own ideology, his most significant contribution was his stripping reality of prejudice, sentiment, emotion, subjectivity in all its forms and ramifications. From this standpoint, the entire first volume could stand as a general introduction to the ideals of science: the quest for complete objectivity. And yet no one denies that in the monumental Paretan edifice there are numerous contradictions, errors and distortions. His impatience with Senator René Bérenger verges on a mania. The same must be stated about his irritability with reference to the censorship of pornographic books and post-cards. His *bête noire* stares at us from a hundred different paragraphs.

"It would be an interesting study in psychology to discover how far his unhappy first marriage affected this attitude or what personal experience made him rage forever after at the thought of any limitations upon the free distribution of obscene pictures. The prolonged, solemn discussion the professor provides about the 'sex residue' would indicate some abnormal preoccupation with the functions of physical love, and force from the translator, Professor Livingston, this unconsciously humorous comment: 'In his treatment of the sex residue Pareto is less objective than is his wont'. In other words, the Olympian detachment of the Philosopher of the Non-logical remains an aspiration and an unfulfilled hope."

"All in all, Father Walsh, would you think it worth while to plough through Pareto three or four times?"

"It is a treatise that every educated, cultured citizen of the world should know. You need not lavish on it the nine-thousand hours of patient toil which Professor Livingston devoted to the translation over a period of fifteen years. Nor would I recommend that you rush through it in the seventy-eight hours which John Chamberlain, one-time book-review editor of the *New York Times,* asserts is the time necessary to peruse the whole text. It is, in its own sphere and subject to the limitations suggested in this interview, a valuable book of reference. It will find its way into most libraries and the serious student of society will quarry from the granite rock of its heterogeneous material numerous enlightening examples and, if not devoid of a sense of humor, many a quiet chuckle at the spectacle of a synthesis of universal knowledge that quite overlooks the real arbiter of human destinies: the power and faculty of man, with the grace of God, to reject evil and to choose good."

CHAPTER IV

THE JOCISTS

Pioneers of the New Social Order

THE WAR in Europe has not changed the need for rebuilding our social order with a view to justice for the workingman. Indeed, a fair deal for the workers will do much to remove the causes of conflict. Consequently, every move that puts wealth and income into the hands of the laboring population is an advance on the road to world peace.

Prior to the World War in 1914, a start had been made in Belgium to give the workingman his due. Like war, it began in tragedy. The drama was one of labor organization and its leading character was a young man named Joseph Cardijn, born on November 13, 1882. This youngster had held the crucifix to the lips of his father, whose death, in the full blush of manhood, was attributable to toil in a factory where unsanitary conditions prevailed. Watching the agonized features of his dying father, Joseph Cardijn made a pledge that he would devote his life to a crusade for health and happiness among the working people of Belgium. This pledge was repeated and consecrated by a vow he made upon

33

the eve of his promotion to the sacred Order of the Priesthood. That was in June, 1906.

THE PRELUDE

Before plunging into the task of unionization, Father Cardijn studied the subject at home and abroad. A trip to the factory districts of England brought him into touch with the British Trade Union movement. Returning to Belgium, he was given a short teaching assignment in the archiepiscopal college and was then appointed curate at the Church of Our Lady at Laeken.

Again, his technique was one of investigation and study, this time on a cooperative basis. In conjunction with "a few high-minded men" he brought to light the vicious conditions which prevailed in the workshops and factories of the neighborhood. Filth accumulated in the washrooms and toilets. Rest-rooms for young women workers were non-existent. Pay was scanty; hours long. Both the health and morals of boys and girls were in peril.

Home life did little to counteract the bad influence of mine and shop. The majority of the workers infested, rather than lived in slum districts that reeked with the odor of clogged drains and uncollected garbage. Was it surprising that the young priest decided that his first job was to create a healthy mental attitude among his parishioners and, more particularly, to help the youth of both sexes to overcome the inferiority complex which, in the haunts of poverty, bred with the speed of weeds in a swamp? He determined that his people should learn to help each other.

In 1912, therefore, Father Joseph Cardijn gathered together the nucleus of a labor organization with spiritual ideals: seven needleworkers, all girls and all between the ages of thirteen and fourteen. Presently their numbers were augmented by a group of young men, eager to better their own condition and that of their fellow workers. *Piety, Study, Action* were the original watchwords of this little band.

ORGANIZATIONAL BEGINNINGS

The year 1915 was a turning-point in a two-fold sense: a syndicate of apprentices was formed and the fury of the World War swept through the ranks of the young organization. Many members of the syndicate were mobilized; some were killed; others were wounded and allowed to return to their home communities. Father Cardijn continued his work with the few who remained or returned. These four years were a period of intensive training and preparation.

At the end of the conflict in 1919, the stage was set for a genuine youth labor organization called the Youth Syndicate. The next year, five priests, inflamed by zeal for the cause, joined the movement. Hundreds of workers flocked to the standard of Christ the Worker and a newspaper was founded with the banner headline: *Young Syndicalist Workers.* The campaign was blessed by Archbishops and Bishops. Benedict XV in Rome added his august commendation. Finally, the movement crystalized in 1924 as the *Jeunesse Ouvrière Chrétienne,* more popularly known as the Jocists. Youth in action for the workers, under religious auspices and motivation, tells the whole story in a nutshell.

THE SPIRIT

"Back to Christ, Young Workers!" constituted the rallying cry of the Jocists. They were organized according to their vocational set-up: the students with students; chemists with chemists; transport workers with transport workers; and farmers with farmers. Badges and uniforms were distributed; meetings were held; study circles developed for weekly conferences; and public manifestations prepared.

See, Judge, Act became the order of procedure. The inquiry precedes every other task. Mr. Paul McGuire calls it the "nerve center of the whole Jocist method." The young worker observes and collects concrete facts which show the real position of the wage earner and his responsibility. In the study circles he discusses these facts with his comrades; together they look for the causes of a given evil and its opposition to the plan of God as revealed in the Gospel. When the moment comes for action, the young laborers choose a remedy; they help a companion who is out of work, sick or injured, or a worker's family; or they assist some one of their members in the choice of a profession or further vocational training. Each section provides facilities for thrift, insurance, credit unions, labor organization and moral education.

The atmosphere of a secretariat is electric with plans, ideas and accomplishments. The movement, working on the imaginations of the youthful members, creates a mass psychology which inspires courage and confidence in the ranks of labor. In these circles the carpenter or miner feels himself better understood, more firmly upheld and more fervently loved. In short, the youth of all classes are fired with blazing enthusiasm for the world of tomorrow which is to be their world. *Conquest for*

Christ is dramatized as the work of *A New Youth for a New World.*

GROWTH AND EXTENSION

When Father Joseph Cardijn visited Rome in 1925, he was received by His Holiness, Pius XI. The Pope gave His paternal blessing to the Jocists. In the same year, the group of needleworkers who had organized in 1912 adopted the name of *Jeunesse Ouvrière Chrétienne Feminine;* the first national committee of the J.O.C. was formed; a general Congress was convoked in Brussels, and in October the *Jocist Manual* was published. By the end of 1926, the Beligan experiment had not only established itself in every parish of the nation, but also had attracted attention in neighboring countries.

Early in 1927, Father Cardijn was invited to the so-called Red Zone of Paris, a Communist stronghold, in order to familiarize the French workers with the apostolic nature of the Jocist organization. The first meeting was held in the dingy room of one of the Parisian clergy. Seven hundred young workers were invited to an organizational meeting; seventy accepted. A young layman explained the Belgian activities; what their brothers and sisters were trying to accomplish across the border; what they believed could be done in France. Six workers were interested enough to enroll themselves in the unit. Within two years there were one hundred and ten similar centers.

Five years later, there were five hundred active units in the Parish community alone. The national organization counted sixty thousand workers. The Young Christian Peasants (J.A.C.) have an equally large organization, recruited from the sons and daughters of farmers and farm laborers. Forty thousand French students from universities, colleges, high schools, technical and primary schools are united in a movement called the J.E.C. (the Young Christian Students), while the youth of independent groups are gathered in the J.I.C. (Youth of the Middle Class). Each member has the zeal of an apostle, influencing the lives of at least ten of his work-mates or fellow clerks, or fellow students. Every Jocist develops religious and social reform at his or her own point of contact with the world. In this way, the leaven of Christ permeates every environment, or *milieu,* from the mines to the shops and stock exchange.

Christ's Presence

Why should a single worker be able to radiate virtue, power, joy?

The answer is to be sought in the individual Jocist's sense of the presence of God. Christ is present to these workers in His name. Their minds and their hearts are lifted on high. Religion is the familiar stuff of their lives. Aware of Christ's teaching, they talk of their Leader with the intimacy and ease with which boys and girls speak of their adventures, their amusements, their picnics, their playmates or their jobs. Not that these activities are the be-all and end-all of existence: they are but episodes in lives that are meant to be wholly Catholic. If one goes motoring, Christ is in the car.

Daily life is conceived of as a vocation: a complete life; a thorough destiny; writing, studying, games, work, dancing, scouting, courtship, marriage, entertaining or being entertained . . . all these are dipped in the chrism of Christ stamped with the seal of Christ, blazing with the love of Christ. Or, to use Paul McGuire's happy phrase, all these routines of daily existence are "Christened," vitalized by the heart-beats of God. This is more than Strength through Joy: it is union with the Fountain-head of Grace, Virtue, and Eternal Glory.

Is it any wonder that the *Revue Des Jeunes* (Paris) can write: "After attending some J. O. C. meetings one realizes what gigantic progress it is making toward the rechristianization of the working classes." Besides direct contact work, J. O. C. employs songs, movies, pamphlets, picnics, public manifestations. It conducts vocation and orientation service while other functions include measures to secure work, board and legal advice for members or non-members. It gives assistance to soldiers and sailors, furnishes medical aid, rehabilitation services, and nursing care. Of course, the backbone of these services is a network of syndicates, savings banks and insurance systems.

The song of the Third Communist International intones the melancholy refrain: "Stand, ye damned of the earth . . . "

In marked contrast to this depressing sentiment is the ringing challenge of the Jocist hymn. This sings out to youth:

> *"Stand, the call of Christ resounds.*
> *The task is noble, but stern.*
> *Onward with the struggle,*
> *Never resting nor relenting,*
> *For Christ we must conquer."*

TENTH ANNIVERSARY

Cannon Joseph Cardijn at the tenth anniversary celebration of his organization, in the presence of 100,000 devoted companions, described the conditions and motives which had inspired him to create the J. O. C. The spiritual growth and temporal life of the young workman, he declared, are inseparable. Further, it is not possible to ignore a man's material life, if one wishes to help him to save his soul; living and working conditions formerly prevailing among workmen were in brutal contradiction to what was necessary to help them gain eternal life; the situation can be mastered only by forming and organizing workers in such a manner that they can help themselves and conquer their own salvation. Speaking of the goal of the J. O. C. he added, in a stirring peroration that brought his audience to its feet:

"Not slaves, not beasts of burden, not machines, but sons, collaborators, heirs of God!

"And to accomplish this there must be work: in the midst of work a center of work and an organization of work;

"And for that there must be a home and family life;

"And for that there must be a professional organization, a social organization, a national and an international organization which must be worthy of this origin divine, of this dignity divine, of this destiny divine.

"The young workers are not destined for material wealth, nor for imperialism, nor for totalitarian nationalism.

"But riches, but work, but economic, and financial organization, but the entire civilization must help all the young workers and the men of the whole world to attain their destinies . . .

"Against atheism, against nihilism, against materialism, the J. O. C. struggles with energy and courage,

with staunch soul and with hearts dedicated to the real
and complete royalty of Christ, guided by the Church,
in the ranks of the Catholic crusade, which groups,
transforms and launches the young workers as apostles
among their brothers and in their centers . . .

"Jocists, be ye the glory of the Church,
Jocists, be ye the glory of Christ,
Jocists, be ye the honor of your country,
Jocists, be ye the hope of your times,
I bless ye,
Forward!"

PROTESTANT TRIBUTE

It may be prudent to balance this enthusiastic valedictory with the report published by a distinguished
Protestant gentleman, Mr. Harold B. Butler, director of
the International Labor Office at Geneva. In the course
of a statement which described the social activities of
the churches, Mr. Butler wrote:

"The social work done by the Catholics tended to
confirm further the supremacy of the moral element
over the economic order, and of man over the product
of his work. Catholic associations realize more and
more that it is useless to establish even the most perfect
organizations, if at the same time the spiritual level is
not raised; in 1934, there was a new movement on these
lines . . . The work done by the Jocists for the improvement of the laboring classes is well known. The spread
of specialization in the important organizations of Catholic Youth is due to the Jocist movement. Thanks to its
example, to its influence, Jocism has made the Papal
instructions, now the standard in social movements,
possible to all: 'The first apostles for the workman, are

to be workmen, and the apostles for the industrial and commercial world, are to be industrialists and merchants' (*Quadragesimo Anno*)."

THE RECKONING

There are 200,000 young men and women organized on these principles in France; 10,000 in Holland; 2,000 in Switzerland and growing centers in Spain, Portugal, Colombia, the Belgian Congo and Great Britain. Prior to the tragic events of the current conflict the movement was being seriously studied with a view to an organization in Catholic Poland. Lithuanian and Czech and Slovak workers had likewise evinced an interest in the movement. Within a relatively short time, the Jocists have enjoyed phenomenal success in Canada, while the United States has witnessed the spread of this Canadian effort in New England.

The Belgian J.O.C. now counts 68 regional federations for boys and girls; 2,204 local sections in some 2,670 cities and villages in Belgium; 85,000 members, divided equally among boys and girls. It must be borne in mind that each of these units has its own publications, served by national magazines and reviews. During 1935, 1,735,320 pamphlets, explaining the social philosophy of the Church were distributed. One workman, who read some of this material, made a typical remark:

"So Christians still exist; for the thirty years I have been working here the only pamphlets I've been given have been distributed by Communists, Marxists or freethinkers. I had never been told that a God died for me." This occurred in the factory of John Cockerill in England.

CANADIAN JOCISTS

Jocism in Canada was introduced, as in France, by a priest, Father Henri Roy, O.M.I., who, like Father Joseph Cardijn, belonged to an impoverished working-man's family. Father Roy, a native of Lewiston, still remembers with a terrible tenseness the days and nights when as a boy of seven he crept out of the Montreal slums to sell newspapers, carry messages, do odd jobs, anything—for a few pennies with which to buy food for the family. In order to study for the Priesthood he undertook a high school course at the age of twenty-two. To-day, he stands in the front ranks of 50,000 Jocists in Canada. His motto remains what it was in the initial stages of his career: "On Guard for Christ, Young Workers!"

At the J.O.C. headquarters in Montreal, consisting of several huge rambling buildings painted red and gray, there is a constant flow of homeless youngsters. Thousands find food, clothing, shelter. Both a doctor and a dentist are on hand to give the young people the care they need.

Every effort is made to find work for both boys and girls. Employers cooperate wholeheartedly with Father Roy, for he has bettered working conditions not only for the youngsters, but also for the employers. Theft, breakage and waste in the factories have been practically eliminated.

"What can you offer your comrades?" one of the Jocists was asked.

"Nothing, but a chance. We spread confidence in God and life everlasting. If the workers do not get what they richly deserve in this life, then in another life they will reap their reward. It is Eternal Hope, my friend, that makes the world go round and keeps us steadfast."

In July, 1938, the Canadian Jocists gave a practical and singular exhibition of their philsophy and Faith. One Sunday, in the Cathedral of Notre Dame, Montreal, 106 couples were united in Holy Matrimony. The streets were filled with boys and girls in blue and white uniforms with blue berets and the prized J.O.C. pins. Inside the Cathedral, thousands upon thousands of youthful voices were lifted in song. It was the greatest mass marriage ever celebrated on this continent. It was a triumph of tomorrow over the divorces, childless marriages, contraceptives and indecencies of today.

JOCISTS IN THE U.S.A.

A most interesting study of American Jocism has been undertaken by Mr. Paul J. Taggart, former President of the Student Council at Mt. St. Mary's College, Emmitsburg, Maryland. According to Mr. Taggart, who visited Jocist headquarters at St. Marie, Sacred Heart and St. Augustin parishes in Manchester, New Hampshire, the secret of the J.O.C. "Miracle" is hard work and intelligent use of time by young Catholic workers. He describes a meeting in which "the youths are all primed" with knowledge and questions. The Jocist, he relates, "prays" . . . "attends retreats" . . . "frequents the Sacraments" . . . "begins his work soundly entrenched in Catholic practice as well as Catholic principles."

Mr. Taggart describes as typical the success of a few Jocists in a shoe factory who managed to quiet the filthy tongues of their fellow workers. Many workers objected to indecent speech and impure topics of conversation, but it took a few Jocists to put their foot down—by their pure example—and clean up a moral cesspool. That won respect for the little band, and now the few are busy teaching the many the inner meaning of Jocism.

Father Achille Lettré, the spiritual director of St. Augustin parish unit, is quoted as follows:

"We would be suspicious of gifts of money. We don't ask for that. We ask for gifts of Self. A man must labor for God before he appreciates Jocism. What we want is work."

In other words, the difference between a Communist and a Jocist is that the Communist says to his fellow worker: "What you have is mine," and the Jocist says to his companion: "What I have is yours."

CHAPTER V

DR. HERBERT ELLSWORTH CORY

A Dean of the Pacific Northwest

"EAST IS EAST and West is West, and never the twain shall meet!" is an epigram that doesn't apply to America. Least of all, is it applicable to one of the most distinguished converts to Catholicism in the last ten years, Dr. Herbert Ellsworth Cory, dean of the Department of Liberal Arts at the University of Washington, Seattle. This American scholar, although now a resident of the Pacific Northwest, within hailing distance of Puget Sound, was born in New England. His parents were descendants of the early Puritans, who landed in Boston and then migrated to Providence, Rhode Island. It was in this town, in the year 1883, that Herbert Cory saw the light of day.

Cory's early education was Congregationalist at home and very, very English at the famous Peace Street grammar school in Providence. A taste for Latin and Greek learning was acquired at Providence Classical High School. Dean Cory still believes that there is no better foundation for life than a thorough grounding in the Iliad and Odyssey. The classical tradition was maintained at Brown University where the young scholar

46

took his Bachelor of Arts degree in 1906. The next four years were devoted to graduate studies in English Literature at Harvard University. When Cory was awarded his Ph.D. at Cambridge, Massachusetts, in 1910, he seemed to be following the familiar pattern of a regular 'Down Easter.

The college years, however, wrought a marked religious change. As a child Herbert Ellsworth Cory had been a member of the Congregationalist Church. His memories of life in that denomination are pleasant. His fellow parishioners were kindly, gracious folk who, unlike their Puritan forbears, looked with tolerance upon card playing, dancing and an occasional glass of wine or beer. Rhode Island retained a good deal of the liberal spirit of Roger Williams. Consequently, Dr. Cory can testify that his Congregationalist faith, though without a deep rational basis, was "free from the bigotry and Puritanical angularities which mar so many Protestant beliefs."

In this connection, Mr. Cory makes a most interesting observation. "Most of my colleagues in non-Catholic universities," he reports, "have been subjected to much more vinegar-visaged versions of Protestantism. In consequence, they are only too glad to get rid of the last vestiges of the faith of their fathers, and I do not in any degree blame them; but they go on to make the unpardonable mistake of supposing that all religions must be essentially the same as the religion which they were taught: that religion must be founded in fear, in the racketeering of some priestcraft; that it is a survival of barbarism, and is of its very nature hostile to all progress.

"In my own case, the faith which was given to me, though vague, was at least kindly. When, therefore, I found myself without it, I sorrowed as one who had lost the dearest of friends, and my life became intensely restless, highly adventurous in all fields of learning, a fact which will explain a good many of my subsequent experiences."

Truth to tell, young Cory's religious convictions crumbled at the first contact with the discoveries of the natural sciences. Reversing the dictum of Saint Paul, the Apostle of the Gentiles, Dr. Cory was shocked as well as stunned to see that his faith was not a "rational service." The tombstone was rolled on the grave of his beliefs by a specialized study of skeptical literary men. His dream of the brotherhood of man was punctured by the gentle satire of a number of the great Victorian poets and essayists. He was like a New England clipper ship with a full spread of canvas and no rudder.

Nevertheless, there were lights on the shore beckoning to the true harbor. Cory's mother, who was something of a religious eclectic (the son himself sometimes thought of her as an "ecclesiastical gypsy"), loved to venture into the churches of all denominations and of the most diverse worship. Occasionally, she took her boy to some Catholic chapel or to the Providence Cathedral. Her lodestar was Rome, as her son repeatedly declared. The direction of her thoughts may be judged from the fact that Mrs. Cory, outgrowing her Congregationalism, was received into the Anglican communion and was about to receive instructions in Catholicism when God took her to her reward. But she had lived long enough to introduce her son to the sources of the Faith and to put him in touch with the beauties of the Catholic liturgy.

Strange to relate, Dr. Cory, who unabashedly told his mother that Rome was her logical goal, was reluctant to study the credentials of Catholic Christianity. He does not hesitate to acknowledge that he may have resisted powerful graces. Preoccupied with beauty in literature, sculpture, painting and architecture, the youthful scholar was fearful that he might be influenced by the externals of Divine service and enter the Church by the portal of Chateaubriand. Listening to César Franck's great Symphony in the shadow of the lovely spires of the Cologne Cathedral, he retired to rest with the following soliloquy on his lips:

"If Catholicism can inspire a man to write music like that, it must contain an enormous measure of truth."

This esthetic appeal of historic Christianity was reinforced by Cory's love of the poetry of the gifted English Catholics from Cynewulf to Crashaw, and from Crashaw to Frances Thompson. There was more than a passing analogy in the latter's *Hound of Heaven* and the questing love of the Saviour in Cory's own spiritual Odyssey.

At this point in his career, Cory was introduced to Catholic books, magazines and periodicals by a devoted Catholic friend, Ellen Virgin. To his amazement, the young seeker after truth discovered that no Jesuit taught that the end justified the means. On the other hand, he found out that Josef Stalin and the Soviets were the foremost exponents as well as practitioners of this doctrine! "The Popes and Science" by Dr. James J. Walsh and a number of pamphlets published by the International Catholic Truth Society brought home to

Cory that the Church has been and remains a staunch friend of scientific research. Fortunately, he likewise remembered, from his study of medieval literature in its original dialects, that the monastic centers had been the best repositories of culture and learning during the so-called "Dark Ages." Investigation of the high "Middle Ages," the ages of Faith, persuaded him that the supreme achievement of Christian civilization had been an age of genuine enlightenment.

In spite of the richness of this intellectual approach, Dr. Cory, as he himself now puts it, showed a "fear of the sinister influence of the 'wish-to-believe' that was almost pathological."

West called East in 1910 and Cory, fresh from his studies at Harvard, accepted a teaching assignment in the English Department of the University of California. During the eight years at Berkeley, the young instructor continued his "restless search for some rock of ages." The spiritual wrestling manifested itself in two distinct ways: first, by an omnivorous gulping of university courses in philosophy, economics, sociology, political science; and, secondly, by participation in the more radical phases of the labor movement.

Twin stars shone on the academic horizon: Hegel with his idealistic pantheism and Karl Marx with his religion of humanity and revolution. As the size of the German philosopher of Prussianism dwindled, the stature of Marx, the prophet, gained new dimensions. Yet it irked Cory that his idol should be fashioned of the clay of materialistic atheism. In an abortive effort to spiritualize Marx and his followers, he wrote what he himself calls "a romantic little volume" entitled *The*

Intellectuals and the Wage Workers. This was the signal for an invitation to join the so-called Guild Socialists of England. Like many idealists in the Marxian ranks, he cherished "the Rousseauistic notion that the rebellious emerging proletariat would become more and more spiritual as they drew nearer and nearer their goal." To offset his "proletarian rhapsodizing," Dr. Cory kept plugging away at his English research and in 1917 produced *Edmund Spenser, A Critical Study,* a volume that still rates high with scholars in the field.

New England and the East made an emergency call on the West in August, 1918. An invitation came from the Government in Washington to join Professor Felix Frankfurter's War Policy Board. The capital was crowded with war workers and no one had to labor overtime. Cory decided to utilize his leisure by commuting to Baltimore two or three times a week in order to undertake biological and psychological research in the laboratories of Johns Hopkins University. He wanted his notions of social science to take firm root in the exact technique of Biology.

While in the East Dr. Cory had a chance to make some close-up observations of American radicals like Max Eastman and Scott Nearing. His conclusion was that most bell-wethers of the Left wing labor movement were "unconsciously much more egoistic than altruistic." In short, they seemed to be making a good business of idealism. Furthermore, and what is probably more important, the questing radical detected "impurity of heart" in himself. At this point, his own confession is edifying:

"My revolutionary religion went the way of my Congregationalism and I was left spiritually bankrupt."

The death of his beloved Mother in 1920 was another blow. In the first shock of grief Cory determined to resign his position at the University of California and to spend his lean patrimony on some extended research in the laboratories of Johns Hopkins. What his objective in the search was he did not pretend to know. It was simply his conviction that truth must lie at the end of the quest. God could hardly have been described as the goal of his striving since, as he admits, his "agnosticism had hardened into a sort of hypothetical atheism."

Then, just as the abyss of spiritual surrender yawned, the unexpected happened. Under the microscope and in every alembic gleamed sparks of the Divinity. The student, who had imagined that the *coup de grace* to every rational proof for the existence of God had been delivered by Immanuel Kant, became overwhelmed by awe to find that scientific experimentation invariably and inevitably disclosed *a posteriori* evidence for the reality of the fact of an Infinite Person. The test-tube pointed to Heaven as unerringly and triumphantly as the spires of the *Dom* in Cologne!

The fires of the laboratory had rekindled the flame of art. Again, beauty leaped up from the coals. The argumentation for the existence of a Supreme Being described by St. Thomas Aquinas as the Fifth Way proved the inspiration for a book on Aesthetics. With the humility of a novice Dr. Cory did not embalm the manuscript in a cedar chest to follow the Horatian advice about seven years' maturing in silence. Tossing the pages of his book into the wastebasket, he began once more to struggle with the relation of beauty to reality, the ontological status of the *Splendor Veri,* the Splendor of Truth indicated by Plato. Unwittingly, he was rough-hewing the outline of a persuasive theistic proof which he could later recognize as the magnificent, precise reasoning revealed in St. Thomas' Fourth Way. The Hound of Heaven had triumphed!

In 1923, Dr. Cory was invited to inaugurate at the University of Washington a series of courses which were to help students to gain their intellectual bearings. The purpose was to supply an antidote to premature specialization. Two undergraduate courses were organized: one drawing its materials from the most recent discoveries in natural science, and the other a comparative study of the arts. It was recognized that the goal and unifying principle of these courses would necessarily be a vaguely outlined theistic philosophy.

One of the students who took this course was a young man studying for the Priesthood, Mr. James B. McGoldrick. The latter is now dean of Seattle College. As Father McGoldrick, the young Levite received Dr. Cory into the Catholic Church. The University of Washington savant, by a most painful trial and error method, had grounded himself in the *philosophia perennis* of St. Thomas Aquinas. And from the truths of philosophy to the supernatural revelation of the *Summa Theologica* and the *Summa Contra Gentiles* was not a lyric leap.

In 1922, Dean Cory had married Ethel Morton, who died ten years later. A second marriage was contracted with Mary Ellen Maloney Austin of Juneau, Alaska. Her husband is emphatic in stating that, although Mary Ellen provided rich, superior inspiration, she did not exercise "the slightest explicit influence" in the process of conversion. The couple, in the true Christian spirit, lacking children of their own, have seen fit to adopt five lads and lassies: Michael, Brigid, Mary Sharon, Anthony Francis and James Patrick. They make home! Each one of these little waifs came from one of the orphanages of Blessed Mother Frances Xavier Cabrini, in Seattle.

Obviously, Dean Cory is a leader who loves his fellow man. It is not matter of astonishment to hear that he keeps open house for the young men and women of Seattle, whether they are matriculated in the University or not. Most of these guests are agnostics, "hungering in these days of crushing tension for manna from Heaven." Theirs is a thirst which can only be quenched at the fountain-head of God.

In a household pulsing with rich, warm humanity, the University of Washington professor finds time to continue work on a book to be called *The Drift and Mastery in Contemporary Thought*. It will suggest that most of the recent scientific findings are oriented toward Aristotelian Thomism, the philosophy which is ever ancient and ever new. Dean Cory hopes that this study will fit the capstone on his lifelong building of an arch of Aesthetics. The humanist, the scholar can still repeat with the immortal Dante Alighieri:

"D'antico amor sentì la gran potenza (I felt the power of my ancient love)."

With respect to the transformation wrought in his interior life by embracing the Faith, Dr. Cory humbly remarks:

"I find myself completely at a loss for words when I even think of attempting to describe my supreme happiness today. But, you will understand perfectly."

CHAPTER VI

GERALD P. NYE

A Champion of Peace — On Munitions

LET ME say at the outset that there was a marked contrast between the office of Senator Gerald P. Nye and that of the Honorable Huey P. Long. In color, tone, and movement the Louisianian's entourage suggested a cross between a carnival and a circus. In other words, Suite 143 in the Senate Office Building had all the earmarks of the headquarters of a pre-season Presidential candidate. Even a glance through the open windows of Senator Long's office revealed the constant ebb and flow of traffic around the Columbus Monument in front of the crowded Union Station. On the other hand, the rooms of Senator Nye, faintly reminiscent of the cloistered peace of an Oxford college, looked out upon the greensward of a quiet quadrangle. Within and without there was order, dignity and calm, if not contentment.

Senator Nye himself was engaged in study. Before him was a heavy tome on international law. Its title was significant: "Neutrality Laws." An analysis of the profit system as it had been exploited by war merchants apparently had led the Chairman of the Senate

56

Munitions Investigation Committee to see the need of some revision of our neutrality laws, if we were not to be again drawn into the maelstrom of international conflict.

Senator Nye rose from his study to express a cordial greeting to myself and my esteemed colleague, Father George A. McDonald, associate editor of *The Queen's Work*.

"First of all, Fathers," were his after-welcome words, "permit me to assure you that every member of our committee has read and admired the presentation of the munitions problem by Father Paul L. Blakely and Father Laurence Kent Paterson in various Catholic publications. Frankly, we consider these articles and other editorials in your magazines and reviews among the best we have followed on the subject. Each one of us believes that the Senate Committee in its work of research and analysis has had magnificent support from the religious press."

This was an encouraging start for the interview. Without hesitation, this correspondent launched his first question:

"What in your judgment, Senator, is the principal benefit which has been derived from this inquiry?"

The answer was clear and direct:

"I believe," declared the North Dakotan, "that this investigation has established as a fact what has frequently been asserted by rumor. In other words, it is a striking confirmation of numerous suspicions that have troubled the minds of thoughtful, observant men. The letters, telegrams, audited financial statements, confidential instructions to agents and similar documents found in the files of munitions makers have given access to a well-rounded picture of the international munitions ring.

"The 'Secret International' is no longer so much of a secret. As the hearings progressed, this became increasingly evident. The vague accusation of interlocking directorates and division of profits, often founded chiefly on report and emotion, soon emerged as a substantiated indictment. This, to my mind, is a positive, definite gain. We know many things that formerly were merely matters of idle speculation. Equipped with knowledge, we can now weigh the appropriate course of action."

"This is important general information, Senator," I continued. "But I am sure that everybody would be interested to hear what type of evidence most astonished you, who have for many years been a student of the problem of war and peace."

"Well, I was only mildly surprised by our preliminary discoveries," replied Senator Nye. "It did not astonish me greatly to see how wide were the ramifications of the international munitions trust. The interlocking directorates of Vickers-Armstrong, Schneider-Creusot, Skoda, Vickers, Terni, and Mitsui, illustrative as they are of the supra-nationalism of the death industry, did not shock me nearly so much as the association of governmental agencies or departments in the demonstration and sale of armament equipment.

"It is horrifying to find American firms not only eager to sell the raw materials of war, like scrap steel and cotton, to Japan, but also willing to outfit potential rivals with the highly modernized death-dealing arms of latest invention. The fact that these weapons may some day be turned upon Americans does not seem to weigh heavily on the consciences of the directors of these corporations. They are interested in sales and above all profits.

"But this is not the climax. The most shocking phase of the whole sorry business is that these commercial houses can actually secure naval vessels to furnish an exhibit of wares to foreign waters."

"Naval vessels?" I inquired. "Do you mean, Senator, that American warships were put through their pace in trade demonstrations like Fordson tractors and fancy egg-beaters at a country fair?"

For the first and only time in the interview, sparks of fire seemed to flash from Mr. Nye's calm, Nordic-blue eyes.

"I mean United States naval vessels, I mean the United States Navy," he insisted, punctuating his words like rifle shots.

"Could you give one specific example of this practice? You know how curious the public has become about names and places," your correspondent continued.

"Certainly," replied the Senator. "A few years ago, the Driggs type of gun for warships, combining many features of weight and marksmanship, was perfected by an American manufacturer. The latter wanted to increase his sales abroad. Pictures and diagrams of the gun were forwarded to a certain European nation that was interested in armament. Brightly painted pictures did not clinch the sale. The manufacturer tried another prospect. This time it was Turkey. Turkey was attracted by the advertised features of the new gun. Could they not see a sample on the decks of a battleship?

"The salesman, frantic for business, cabled the home office. The home office got in some effective words with the Navy Department. The U.S.S. *Raleigh* was dispatched to Constantinople. Turkish Admirals, Generals, the Minister of War and the numerous personnel of the Marine Ministry were on hand. United States naval officers conducted the demonstration. The gun was a success. Everybody was impressed. The Admirals were delighted. And so the salesman got a spot order to rush goods. The *Raleigh* had clinched the sale."

Since I had heard Senator Nye question Bernard M. Baruch earlier in the week, it occurred to me to ask for some intimate impressions of the place of the latter's testimony in the whole investigation.

"Personalities are always interesting, Senator," I observed. "Would you tell us whether you think Mr. Baruch in his testimony showed a changed attitude toward the problem of war profits?"

The answer was instant, emphatic:

"Mr. Baruch has changed tremendously," declared Senator Nye. "Ten months ago, I think we would have heard quite a different story from the ex-Chairman of the War Industries Board."

"How do you account for this change?"

"In my opinion, it is due to the impact of public opinion. And public sentiment has been crystallized on this question in no small degree by the revelations produced by the work of the Munitions Committee. To tell you the truth, the change is not unlike a peaceful rebellion against the war-profits system. My own mail has grown to huge proportions as a result of the inquiry. Perhaps upwards of 150,000 letters, all intelligent and enthusiastic, have reached me urging the members of the committee to supplement their report by some scientific legislation.

"These correspondents were appalled by the fact that the Du Ponts not only reported a 400 per cent profit on their business during the World War, but also considered this figure a not unreasonable return for prompt, efficient service. Felix Du Pont, you remember, testified that without this timely, telling assistance the United States would have been in a fair way to becoming a German colony. The Prussian Guards, in the words of Mr. Baruch, were invariably pounding at the gates of Pittsburgh."

"The Du Ponts and Mr. Baruch are always interesting, Senator," I interposed, "but could you furnish us with your views about Eugene Grace, President of the Bethlehem Steel?"

The Chairman of the Munitions Investigation Committee paused momentarily, while his face grew very serious. He answered almost in a tone of solemnity.

"Mr. Eugene Grace is only one example of a man living in a world all by himself. Apparently, he has no humanitarian interest, little or no appreciation of the importance of the larger issues of the public interest. His primary, if not his sole, obligation appears to be to the stockholders. The same may be said of others who testified.

"Mr. Grace, in my judgment, would enhance his value to his own corporation and to his country if he would read or re-read the great Papal Encyclicals. I consider these documents the most effective antidote to the spirit of 'profits first' exhibited by several witnesses at this inquiry. May I add that as a non-Catholic I consider the *Rerum Novarum* of Leo XIII and the *Quadragesimo Anno* of Pius XI to be the most magnificent contribution to social and economic reconstruction which it has been my privilege to study? I would almost be inclined to say that His Holiness furnishes the only leadership of unquestionable world-wide authority in our critical struggle to emerge from the problem created by war and avarice."

There was just time for a final question.

"Is the international arms situation, Senator, comparable to that of 1912-14?"

"In my judgment," he replied, "the danger of war is greater than in the early summer of 1914. We can only pray that a similar or even a more horrible catastrophe can be averted. At any rate, we in the United States have no part in that quarrel. That is why I want to amend our neutrality laws. Both in the sphere of neutrality and in the domain of war profits, do not be surprised at the finely spun legal language that has to be employed. We have tried to close up every loophole. It takes an abundance of words and a host of qualifying clauses. My cheeks will be red and the members of the committee will be mortified, if the proposed legislation, when and if enacted, allows room for evasion and subterfuge. This, I trust, will explain the elaborate precautions of the bill."

CHAPTER VII

ISIDRO CARDINAL GOMA Y TOMÁS

Advocate of A Free Spain

GENERALISSIMO Francisco Franco is unsympathetic to the establishment of any foreign political ideology, particularly Naziism, in Spain, Isidro Cardinal Goma y Tomás, head of the Spanish hierarchy, told this correspondent in an interview at the International Eucharistic Congress at Budapest, Hungary.

Cardinal Goma, who is General Franco's counselor and intimate friend, sought to allay the fears of many Americans that General Franco, if victorious, will become the puppet of Hitler and Mussolini. The Cardinal characterized such fears as "entirely unfounded."

"We are Spaniards," he insisted, "neither satellites nor imitators." To one who knew General Franco as he did, he added, it seemed a grave injustice to picture the generalissimo as a miniature *Fuehrer* or *Duce*. He expressed the belief that General Franco had proved himself one of the foremost soldiers of Europe and could prove himself a leading European statesman.

"I offer no predictions on that score, however," he continued, "except to express in the most categorical

63

manner my complete confidence in the Generalissimo's just and Christian outlook. That is one phase on which my convictions are absolute and ineradicable."

Cardinal Goma told of having made personal representations to General Franco against a totalitarian State and the church's teachings upon the evil of such a State. As a devout Catholic, particularly one holding great authority, General Franco, he insisted, would not go contrary to his church in this respect.

While acknowledging that Nazi assistance to Spanish Insurgents had been a vital factor in their success, Cardinal Goma said this debt would be paid by commercial concessions.

He asserted that Nazi propaganda would not be tolerated in Spain. Nazi propagandists had made attempts, he said, but on each occasion their efforts aroused instant resentment from both lay and ecclesiastical authorities.

"It should be noted," asserted the Cardinal, "that Sr. Jimenez Caballero, who boasted of his anti-Semitism and attempted to lead a movement similar to that of Hitler in Germany, was soon arrested, tried and sentenced to jail. Sr. Caballero is a totally discredited would-be Nazi, whose fate is an object-lesson and warning to any other potential 'little Hitlers' in Spain who might be tempted to worship false gods."

His Eminence added that when General Wilhelm Faupel, former German envoy to Spain, allowed his headquarters to become an incipient center of National Socialist propaganda, there were immediate protests on the part of Catholic Church authorities. This prompt action led to the withdrawal of the offending ambassador. The German successor of General Faupel has adopted an attitude of non-interference in the domestic policy of Spain. It was the Cardinal's impression that Spanish Christians were in no mood to forfeit their national or spiritual independence.

What signs of totalitarianism are apparent in the Spanish Government, are, in the Cardinal's opinion, "a natural reaction to the period of indescribable chaos that brought on the Franco counter-revolt."

"Authority, order and discipline were all in abeyance under the so-called Popular Front Government," he went on. "Worst of all was the weakening of public and private morality. General Franco's first task, therefore, was to restore authority, unity and order."

In the circumstances, according to the Cardinal, a military dictatorship was inevitable. In that sense, and that sense alone, he declared, it was correct to speak of totalitarianism in Spain.

"On the other hand, if totalitarianism is employed as the symbol of a philosophical or political system, the Spanish Government cannot be described as totalitarian," he averred. "Our temperament is radically, perhaps hopelessly individualistic. Regimentation of the type prevailing in Italy and Germany, for example, is unsuited to the Spanish love of independent action and free choice. The State should not and cannot overshadow the individual citizen."

At the same time, Cardinal Goma admitted, there are some groups and leaders supporting General Franco who seek a totalitarian government. He minimized the influence of these elements, however, saying they could be disregarded "in any serious discussion of what the genius of the new Spain will produce in the realm of political ideas and methods."

Under the Franco government, he explained, the work of applying the Papal encyclicals on social justice is being rapidly pushed. Some leading authorities even think these encyclicals are having their greatest application in Spain, he declared. "We have barely scratched the surface in our efforts to help the worker and farmer," he went on. "A tremendous amount remains to be done, and General Franco is the man to do it. There is no part of his program in which he has given more specific guarantees and to which he is devoting greater efforts, even in the midst of his countless tasks.

"On my own initiative, I offered these suggestions: first, that the land problem be approached in a realistic spirit requiring equitable apportionment of the resources of great estates; secondly no discrimination among Spanish provinces respecting political liberty.

"In the latter connection Andalusia ought to be on the same juridical basis as Navarre; Aragon on the same footing as Galicia. This implies a policy of no reprisals, no retaliation, which I am praying will be continued by General Franco."

Cardinal Goma expressed confidence in an eventual triumph of these policies.

CHAPTER VIII

JOSEPH P. KENNEDY

An Envoy With Social Vision

ON THE journey from Castellon de la Plana, Spain, through Sargossa, Burgos, San Sebastian, Paris and London to Dublin, Eire, it was possible for this correspondent to stop over for a few days in the capital of the British Empire. The United States Ambassador, Honorable Joseph P. Kennedy, most graciously made time on his crowded calendar to discuss the mounting crisis in world affairs. What follows is an honest account of that conversation, which will always be remembered as delightfully candid, straightforward and marked by a clear vision of the forces that were driving the nations into conflict. Now that Mr. Kennedy is no longer at the Court of St. James, it may be hoped that he will not find this document too revealing.

The American Ambassador to the Court of St. James declared that faith in God must be the basic cure for the ills of dictatorship. "In an age of despotic, personal rule," he stated, "when the liberties of the individual citizen are trampled upon, religion is the last citadel of strength and protection for the human conscience. As long as men and women have the right to worship God

67

as they see fit, they can keep alive their hope in some future for their freedom to think, speak and write in the light of that faith. It is the first and last rampart against tyranny."

Ambassador Kennedy added that his experiences in England had convinced him that the profound religious spirit of the British people made them wary of attempting any adventures into the realm of either Fascism or Communism. "I find no evidence of sympathy for Marxist materialism in any sphere of public life in Great Britain," he asserted. "Every one in governmental circles here as well as in America realizes how complete has been the Soviet failure to provide the 'good life,' about which so much propaganda has been circulated.

"Communism in Russia, if that is what it must be called, has proved to be the bankruptcy of morals, politics and economics. Is there any responsible statesman who claims that the Soviet system has provided a sound economy? It has had time enough in which to make good its pretensions. The sum total of achievement hardly adds up to zero. It is only a paper movement, from the standpoint of social improvement."

It was Mr. Kennedy's view that this utter inadequacy of the Communist program had inclined a number of thoughtful commentators on world affairs to concentrate upon the danger of Fascism. The latter, he intimated, could point to some constructive features in its efforts to secure material progress. This gave dictatorship a genuine appeal to people who may have become impatient at the recurrence or prolongation of the economic crisis. Those who believe in God, however much they may differ in detail, are thinking in terms of spiritual democracy and free social progress.

Tyranny at home and abroad was a fearful price, the Ambassador suggested, to pay for the loss of democratic liberties. "Beautiful, broad highways, public parks, bountiful supplies of cheap food, museums, playgrounds or swimming pools are a poor substitute for the right of self-government. In the English-speaking world we have our share of these material favors and that without any sacrifice of the pleasant privilege of electing our own representatives to places of trust and responsibility. The people always retain a check-rein over their servants.

"What good is a balanced budget in a dictatorial government? The Finance Minister is neither amenable to Parliament nor subject to impeachment. There is little or no debate on his estimates of revenue or expenditure. He is simply the mouthpiece of the dictator's will. It is even possible that his most potent magic is a piece of masterly bookkeeping.

"Long before I ever came to London," Ambassador Kennedy continued, "it was my conviction that there was every reason why the British Empire, with its traditions of democracy, liberty, and property should look upon the Catholic Church as one of its most valuable, trusted friends. The Church stands for everything that is dear to the Anglo-Saxon heart, including the virtues of family life; a modicum of earthly goods; popular sovereignty; stable government; opportunities for peaceful, personal, national, and international progress; the supremacy of morals and law; and the prime importance of religious belief. My sojourn in London tends to confirm my original conviction. To my mind any clash between the government and the exponents of true religion, either here or in the United States, is silly, short-sighted and futile.

"For that reason," the Ambassador went on to say, "I have not hesitated to mention both to his Eminence, Eugenio Cardinal Pacelli (now Pope Pius XII) and to His Eminence, Richard Cardinal Hinsley, my opinion that priests or clergymen should not interfere in matters of partisan politics. It is perfectly understandable that a minister of religion should interest himself in the improvement of the social order, the payment of a living or family wage, or to secure sanitary, healthful conditions of work for the members of his parish. Leo XIII and Pius XI gave a lead in this sphere which is precious and important. It is, however, unwise for a priest or minister or rabbi to tell his people: 'Vote for DeValera! or, Vote for Cosgrave! Vote the Republican ticket! or, Vote for the Democrats!' Wherever anything of this kind has occurred, it has not benefitted the church whose representative ventured out of his proper field. In certain instances the injury has been far-reaching."

"When you mentioned your views on this subject to Cardinal Pacelli and to Cardinal Hinsley," this correspondent questioned, "did you receive any reply?"

"Certainly," flashed the Ambassador's answer without a moment's hesitation, "They both agreed with me."

Ambassador Kennedy spoke most appreciatively of the cordial reception he had been tendered at Edinburgh, Winchester, Boston, and other British towns. His speeches in several cities were widely publicized in the British press. He was also delighted with the result of his visit to Ireland, where Prime Minister DeValera presided at a banquet in his honor.

"Great Britain and Ireland," declared the Ambassador, "are entering a period of mutual respect. The religious idealism which is notable in the two countries, far from acting as a barrier, should serve as an inspiration to lasting friendship. My own religion has always helped me to respect the sincerity and to cherish the good will of other people, whose faith in God or Providence is no less sincere, I am sure, than my own. Nothing would please me more than to find that my service in the U.S. Embassy in London should contribute to better understanding in this respect."

It was interesting to observe that Mr. Kennedy in the midst of his labors in his new office had found leisure to continue his studies upon the need for an expansion of the United States merchant marine. His study was crowded with books on ships and shipping.

Questioned by this correspondent as to the possibility or necessity of alloting contracts for ship-building in foreign countries, the former chairman of the U.S. Maritime Commission smiled and parried with a question of his own.

"Did you notice what happened when I delivered my first blast against the high figures demanded in the original bids for building ships in American dockyards? The shipbuilders immediately reduced their bids by 30%. This amounted to a difference of $500,000 per ship. Does that sound like sound business negotiation or profiteering?"

"Needless to say, unless we initiate a thoughtful building policy now we may easily be trapped by the same war-time conditions that skyrocketed wages, price of materials and contracts in 1917-1918. In that era the cost of steel doubled, trebled, quadrupled. Other costs shot upwards simultaneously. The result is that we are still paying the interest on three billions that we spent in the frantic effort to remedy our inadequate shipping situation. The money we poured out in this race against time for ships that were never used for their original purpose amounted to a sum that would have supported a reasonable, moderate subsidy plan for three centuries. Fifteen to twenty million dollars a year now can do the work of billions later!"

"What are our present shipping needs, Mr. Ambassador," this correspondent asked.

"We imperatively need one half billion dollars for ships at the present moment. This sum could profitably be expended for cargo ships and perhaps 20 combination cargo-passenger vessels. Consequently, the government is once more in the ship-building business.

"The government is now participating in the construction of 33 ships—one of which is a passenger liner (for the U.S. Lines). The others are cargo ships and tankers.

"In my judgment we can profit by our World War experience by adopting one of three following plans, or all three of them in due proportion:*

(1) "To sell ships to private lines on easy terms, e.g., at the price level which is indicated by the cost of the same ships were they to be constructed in foreign ports.

---

*It is interesting to observe that every one of Mr. Joseph P. Kennedy's ideas, expressed on this occasion, was considered worthy of adoption.

In dollars and cents, this would mean that an American ship operator could secure splendid, new vessels, valued in America at two million dollars, for a sum little in excess of one million. Since the down payment could be fixed at 25% of the foreign cost of production, this would mean that the operator would only have to find 15% in cash of what the government is spending in order to secure title to these ships. It sounds like an extremely attractive proposition for the right people.

(2) "To lease these ships to private lines upon the basis of a yearly rent of 5% of the U.S. cost of the lease. In twenty years the company would have reimbursed the treasury for the original cost of production. Obviously, the saving of interest would be in favor of the operating company.

(3) "To operate the ships governmentally. This means that the United States would run its own lines. No one would be required to buy or lease the ships. In some cases, it is probable that this will occur.

"The survey of the U.S. Maritime Commission disclosed the two grave evils from which the shipping industry is suffering: 1. Replacement of obsolete vessels; 2. Labor problem. The two ills are part of the same disease. Since the ships are old, their crew quarters are cramped, stuffy, unsanitary and unhygienic according to modern standards. This not only creates dissatisfaction among competent, conscientious seamen, but also makes it increasingly difficult to recruit a high-class personnel.

"The best elements along the water-front do not want to enlist in a service which calls for living quarters unfit for animals. Ship inspection cannot be strict in the case of boats that saw their best days twenty years ago. With the passionate cry for social justice arising from factories and mines, where legislation has worked wonders for the toiler in the post-war epoch, it is pathetic to find primitive conditions prevailing in a number of outmoded ships. Removal of grievances is the one sure road to elimination of Communistic influence on American ships.

"In fact, the removal of existing grievances is the best national and international social insurance!"

N.B. How to Be a Joe Kennedy

(From the notebook of a Washington correspondent)

"From now on hopeful parents of little boys are going to point morals like this: 'Study your lessons, hang up your coat, polish your shoes, go to Sunday School, eat your spinach, work at little odd jobs after school, always be polite, say your prayers and smile, and maybe someday you'll grow up to be like Joe Kennedy. If you are, you will be graduated from Harvard *cum laude,* be a bank president at twenty-five, manage Bethlehem Steel at twenty-eight, make millions in the stock market before you are thirty, run a chain of theaters, produce motion pictures, build big ships for your country and make over its entire stock exchange, have nine children, a pretty young wife, four huge estates (plus swimming pools), thousands of friends, be an intimate of a President, have Eddie Moore (combination side-partner, confidential secretary, godfather and *duenna*) and represent your country at the most gorgeous court in the world.'

"Mr. Kennedy is even an improvement on Horatio Alger's boy scouts. He's not gone noble while engaged in worthy works. He's even made money light-heartedly. He has always had a lot of fun!"

CHAPTER IX

DR. HEINRICH BRUENING

Who Might Have Saved Europe!

IN THE autumn of 1931, while studying international relations under the general direction of Sir Alfred Zimmern, who holds the Burton chair in that subject at Oxford University, England, this writer received a letter from a friend of Chancellor Heinrich Bruening in Berlin. The friend was Dr. Maria Schlueter-Hermkes, one of the members of the *Goerresgesellschaft* and a leading German intellectual. This lady had been introduced by Father Edgar R. Smothers, at that time a student at the Sorbonne, now professor at West Baden College, West Baden, Indiana. Her message read as follows:

"Der Herr Reichskanzler ist bereit Sie fuer ein Interview zu empfangen sobald Sie wieder in Deutschland sind (The Chancellor of the Reich is ready to receive you for an interview as soon as you shall make another visit to Germany)."

The next day, at nine in the morning, the recipient of this message was at Croydon airfield, outside London, with a reservation on the German *Lufthansa* passenger plane, *Stolzenfels*. After brief stops at Amsterdam and

76

Hanover, the plane sped to the Tempelhof, Berlin, where this correspondent disembarked at four in the afternoon. Within a half-hour, the time and place for the interview had been arranged; the Reich Chancellery (*Reichskanzlerei*) at six in the evening.

It was a week crowded to capacity for Dr. Bruening. He had presided at a full Cabinet meeting, the reception of the Foreign Minister of Italy, Signor Dino Grandi, and the first gathering of the new economic commission under the presidency of Marshal Paul von Hindenburg. The interview, which took place almost entirely in English, lasted more than one hour. Since that time, the writer has conferred with Dr. Heinrich Bruening, Professor of Government at Harvard University, at the homes of friends in New York and Forest Hills, Long Island. What the former Chancellor of the Reich said on these occasions was not for publication — (until happier times.)

This correspondent's first question was rather general:

"When you took office, Your Excellency, you said you felt your chances of bringing Germany through the financial, economic, and political crisis were ten to one against success. Recently in the Reichstag you declared the situation had improved sufficiently since then to make the chances fifty-fifty. What are your reasons for this somewhat more optimistic view?"

"I am glad you say *somewhat* more optimistic view, because I used the expression in the English sense to indicate that the scales might easily tilt one way or the other. We have the worst of the crisis still to face. However, I do feel that the German people are in a better state of mind psychologically. When I became

Chancellor, the people scarcely realized the precarious financial situation. They were living on the illusions of loans and short-term credits. The possibility of a day of reckoning had not occurred to them. Many of the credits, as you know, had not been for productive enterprises. The expenses of government had grown alarmingly.

"My task was to induce the official classes and in many cases the manual workers to accept salary and wage cuts, which are always unpleasant. It was a task of public education. It meant that the people had to be told disagreeable truths. My Government was the first since the War to meet Germany's obligations out of current earnings and not out of borrowed capital. In short, we faced up to reality and risked unpopularity in bringing the German people to do likewise. This was, I may say, equivalent to turning the tide. Although the German people are feeling the hardships and sacrifices entailed by this new policy, they are finally convinced that borrowing and spending are not the supreme functions of government. The elections recently were fought on a program of economies. These economies, buttressed by heavy taxation, were introduced into effect without dangerous strikes or serious disturbances of the public order. Consequently, I feel that the bulk of the German people have shown splendid good will in cooperating with the first Government to lay all the cards on the table and invite friend and foe to verify every fact and figure."

The next question put by the writer concerned the land and agricultural situation, which is considered basic in the recovery of each of the great industrial nations, Great Britain, Germany, and the United States. The Chancellor's eyes brightened as he replied in firm, confident tones:

"The policy of the present Government in the field of agricultural development has brought about a marked decrease in the importation of foodstuffs. Germany is becoming more and more self-sufficient. Not long ago we had to import 3.6 milliard marks worth of agricultural produce. We have reduced this figure to 1.1 milliards for the first eight months of the current year. Every political party in the Reich recognizes the significance and value of this achievement. They all urge the agrarian development as the foundation of Germany's future greatness. Again this represents a strong program of public education.

"The German people, by raising such a percentage of the necessities of life, were able in September of 1930, one of the severest months in the depression, to show a record-breaking export surplus. No one can doubt the good will and effort embodied in such accomplishment. Furthermore, it should be remembered that these results were attained in face of falling world prices for meat and grain, which tended to impoverish the small farmer. In many cases it meant a stinted diet and short rations, as is clear from the fact that the average consumption of meat in the Reich is three-quarters of a pound per family each week.

"On the other hand," the Chancellor continued, "there is a danger in stimulating export trade in this ratio. Pouring goods into the markets of the world in order to pay private and public debts is apt to disorganize world economy and tend not to the enrichment but the impoverishment of peoples. Events have proved that abnormal production or consumption in any important area tends to have powerful repercussions throughout the globe. One nation does not prosper at the expense of others; nor does one country suffer without tremors of sympathetic pain communicating themselves to neighboring States. The world is one vast economic organism, whose functions are closely interrelated."

Knowing the close relationships between industry and government in the Reich, the reporter asked Dr. Bruening whether there would be any changes of policy in this respect. His answer drew a sharp distinction between large and medium-scale industries:

"Hitherto the Government has been preoccupied almost exclusively with the development of the larger industrial concerns. Foreign credits have been secured chiefly for big combines. Consequently they have benefited from internal and external support. Now our program is to help the middle-class producer and trader. A durable system of private property depends largely on this group. The Government's prompt action in the banking crisis preserved the savings of countless small proprietors and producers. The German people, by their calmness and self-possession in the same crisis, gave indispensable support to the Government's action. It was a transaction which involved 300,000,000 marks, and shouldered the Government with a tremendous responsibility, but it was worth all that to save the financial and economic fabric of German business.

"The protection and development of smaller industries should stimulate internal trade and lift the purchasing power of the German people from its present low ebb.

Combined with the program of agrarian progress it should reduce unemployment. Side by side with a stable currency, to secure lower prices, lower rents and lower production costs is our immediate task."

As the discussion concerned the positive side of Germany's condition, it seemed natural to inquire whether Dr. Bruening looked upon the success of the State railway loan as a sign of renewed confidence and hope. This loan had been proposed on most favorable terms, offering a complete amnesty to those Germans who had evaded the financial decrees of the Reich, and bearing tax exemptions of an extremely attractive type in a country which has had to face the most crushing duties of modern times. At the first floating of the loan, the promoters had been very cautious, allotting contracts for only 100,000,000 marks. By the date the amnesty period closed, almost 200,000,000 had been subscribed. The Chancellor considered this a good return and calculated that it would give whole or part-time employment to at least 100,000 men, besides providing improved equipment, rolling stock, and road-bed for the State railways. There had been a genuine need for this work.

This led the interviewer to ask whether, in the event that the reparations question were settled satisfactorily, Germany's recovery would be prompt and sure. If all clouds had been suddenly swept from the German political sky, the Chancellor could not have looked more pleased.

"Of course," he added, "that would depend on the terms of settlement. The gravity of the present situation is that we must meet 26 milliard marks of long and short term indebtedness with interest and amortization charges, besides the huge burden of reparation payments. Had not President Hoover taken prompt and generous action, it is hard to say what a catastrophe might have occurred. The German people will never forget that act of friendship. The collapse of German credit would not have stopped short of German boundaries. Germany is still the heart of Europe. That is the central fact in the reparations problem."

In conclusion, the Chancellor declared:

"When a great nation has had nothing but new sufferings and new humiliations, it is no longer easy to speak of patience, economy, and self-sacrifice. War, inflation, and debt payments have left their marks on the German psychology. The challenge to sharper sacrifices and sterner self-discipline cannot be repeated or prolonged indefinitely. The time has come to apply adequate far-reaching remedies to the world's ills."

CHAPTER X

GETULIO VARGAS

Brazil's Franklin D. Roosevelt

WHAT MANNER of man is Getulio Vargas? What is the nature of his program for Brazil? How extensive are the ramifications of Fascism, Naziism and Communism in South America? To what degree are politics affected by trade, finance and race? These were among the questions that presented themselves to my mind as the Neptunia, packed to the limit with refugees from central Europe, raced from Trieste in Italy to Rio de Janeiro in Brazil.

The best answer to the first question came from a veteran American newspaperman. He declared:

"President Vargas is the South American counterpart of Franklin D. Roosevelt. He is the smartest politician south of the equator, familiar and fluent in speech with a smile as ready and radiant as the grin of F.D.R. Like the latter the Brazilian chief executive has undeniable talents for publicity and popularity. He is most at home in an audience with members of the press or in attendance at a song-fest of boys and girls. You don't see him surrounded by *élite* guards or strapping secret police. He loves the substance, not the glittering habiliments of

83

power. And like the occupant of the White House in Washington he doesn't show much inclination to relinquish authority."

HIS PRESIDENTIAL CAREER

This reminded me that President Getulio Vargas had come into office in 1930, and that, in November, 1937, when his acute political judgment told him that the forthcoming elections might produce a turnover, he promptly enacted a *coup d'état* that ensconced him more securely in the presidential chair. Once the elections had been postponed *sine die,* Señhor Vargas not only announced the promulgation of a new constitution, but also electrified the country with a series of swiftly executed reforms that had been needed for years and in which the majority of Brazilians found abundant satisfaction. The result is that he has recouped much of the popularity which seemed to be fading rapidly in the autumn of 1937.

At the outset of the November *coup d'état* the impression in many foreign countries, including the United States, was that Brazil had taken a nose dive into the Fascist orbit of power. It was suspected that the Brazilian Nazis, called Green Shirts or *Integralistas* had played a part in the Vargas suspension of constitutional government. A number of foreign critics were even disposed to speak of the *régime* as a thinly disguised Nazi dictatorship which would throw off the mask at an opportune moment.

This impression was strengthened by the boastful utterances of a number of German propagandists and financial agents (pay-off men) who were circulating freely in the southern states of Santa Catherina and Rio

Grande do Sul. The fact that German financial experts had elaborted an ingenious plan to promote the purchase of Brazilian products by means of blocked marks was another element in the situation.

Viewed in the perspective of November, 1938, it would appear that the explanation of what really occurred is much simpler than that outlined in the above analysis. *Integralistas* under the energetic leadership of Plinio Salgado, a gifted intellectual, had succeeded in convincing many more than Getulio Vargas that their movement was a force to be reckoned with in any electoral campaign of revolutionary action in the streets. Politicians, who thought in terms of votes and numbers, began to believe that the only way to deal with a group as large as that led by Salgado was to come to an amicable understanding. In ward politics in the big cities of the United States this is sometimes described as "hitting off a deal."

NAZI HOPES

On the morning of November 10, 1937, therefore, it is quite possible that the Nazis had some reason to believe that the *coup d'état* would in some measure resemble the "bloodless" revolution of Hitler in 1933 or the magnificent pageant of Mussolini's March on Rome. Neither hope was justified. Something happened between rosy dawn and curfew hour!

It is just to inquire what caused this sudden transformation. What were the forces that turned a widely heralded *Integralista* victory into a pulverizing defeat?

The first blow to Nazi hopes was the impact of world opinion, especially the cool, reserved reception of the new régime in London, Paris and Washington. It is to be presumed that the United States Ambassador to Brazil, Honorable J.H. Jefferson Caffery, followed the situation with his usual diligence and skill. Within a few hours it was announced that a statesman of pronounced democratic views, Dr. Oswaldo Aranha, would head the foreign office in the Vargas administration.

This won instantaneous, whole-hearted approbation in responsible circles in Washington. From that moment the orientation of Brazil was away from totalitarianism, dictatorship and arbitrary rule. The *Integralistas* were suppressed; new measures were adopted to combat the communistic agitation; and foreign propaganda was brought under strict control.

Furious at this set-back the Brazilian Nazis, mostly young, irresponsible elements who did not know the dangerous potentialities of their own movement, determined to wreak vengeance upon President Vargas. Last May they came within an ace of assassinating the clever politician who, in their estimate of things, had "run out on them and double-crossed his best friends."

Is This a Dictator?

The conspirators and would-be murderers failed ignominiously. President Vargas, unwilling to create martyrs for a dying cause, left his enemies to the courts, where the verdicts in no instance exceeded imprisonment for eight or ten years. It was significant that the Foreign Secretary of Brazil could tell me that Plinio Salgado, after a short exile in Argentina, is now living quietly in the State of Sao Paulo. True to the Portuguese tradition of moderation and clemency, Vargas does not believe in reprisals.

Obviously, this is not a description of the policy of a dictator. It is easy to imagine what would happen to heedless youths detected in an attempt to murder Hitler, Mussolini or Stalin. Since May, 1938, President Vargas has consolidated his power without resorting to violence, espionage or terror. His program is frankly one of national unification. This calls for vigorous leadership and a strengthening of the federal government at the expense of the states. Anyone who knows the geography and problems of Brazil will agree that this is a much needed reform. A well-known banker in Rio de Janeiro brought this out in the following illustration:

"Our institution in the capital sent out a bill for collection in an outlying section of the Amazon country. It arrived at its destination after three months. That suggests that an excessive concentration of power in the central government is not going to be realized in this generation."

His Own Words

In order to explain his position to me President Vargas used the following words:

"The authority of the government in this matter, is equivalent to a sort of spontaneous delegation of power by the nation. In my capacity as chief of the nation I am encouraged by the proofs of the solidarity of the whole of Brazil."

Then, in order to make sure that he did not want Brazil ranked either as a dictatorship or as one of the totalitarian states, he added:

"Man is not an abstraction of the old formulas, but a living entity, tangible, with hopes, interests, needs, and a definite place in the forefront of the democracies which are seeking to reconcile purely political principles with the demands of the economic system. The social legislation of Brazil not only carries out our duty to aid our working classes, but also strengthens the structure of the state, giving it strength, dignity and authority."

If you close your eyes and meditate on this statement, you can easily imagine it pronounced by a silken voice which issues from the hearth-side microphone installed in the mansion on Pennsylvania Avenue. "Uncle Getulio" is the Brazilian F.D.R. Due to Señhor Vargas' success in tightening up the gears and rivets on the Brazilian national machines, both political and economic, Jim Marshall, feature writer of *Collier's,* calls Vargas "the man with the screw-driver." But in the hearts and minds of most Brazilians he is still "Uncle Getulio." Does it point a contrast to recall that nobody has ever been prompted to refer to Mussolini or Hitler or Stalin as "Uncle Ben," or "Onkel Adolf," or "Uncle Josef"? On the other hand, it would not be in the least startling to hear "the Country Squire in the White House" described as "Uncle Frank!"

CHAPTER XI

GETULIO VARGAS

How Brazil Conquered Communism

THERE is one country in the world where Marxist Communism, if not actually defeated, is completely on the defensive. That nation is the United States of Brazil. Its President is Getulio Vargas and his program is openly proclaimed as "the overthrow of subversive elements."

How was atheistic materialism overcome in the largest and most populous South American republic? This was the subject of my recent conversation with Señhor Getulio Vargas in the Cattete palace at Rio de Janeiro.

The chief executive on this occasion fully lived up to his sobriquet of "Uncle Getulio." His attitude was gracious, cordial, candid. Answering questions without a moment's hesitation, he gave the impression of a public official who was eager to place his national policies in their proper light before the world.

My first inquiry to Mr. Vargas concerned the menace of Marxism in Brazil. With flashing eyes the President replied:

"In 1930 the danger of Marxism was very real. World economic conditions naturally affected the standard of

89

living in our country. The Communists, supported by other Leftist groups, tried to exploit this situation. Their propaganda and their agitation extended into the most remote provinces of Brazil. Our huge population, to a large extent unprotected by social legislation, was particularly exposed to extremist attacks. Forty-seven million people, spread throughout a nation larger than the United States of America, were regarded by the emissaries of Moscow as a rich plum for the South American Soviet Union!"

THE CAMPAIGN AGAINST COMMUNISM

President Vargas then explained the manifold nature of his campaign against Communism. He enumerated three distinct phases in his battle against Stalinism: (1) prompt development of a broad program of social justice, thus eliminating the grievances upon which communistic agitation feeds; (2) scientific counter propaganda, which drew its most persuasive power from the measures of actual reform initiated by the government; (3) energy and determination in crushing armed violence by military and police vigilance.

Each one of these three activities, the Brazilian President insisted, was essential. It was his view that social reconstruction was the fountain-head of the benefits that put the workers and farmers in a mood to heed the national propaganda, which was conspicuous on billboards as well as on the walls of public buildings. As an illustration of his interest in the cause of adequate defense, Mr. Vargas cited increased appropriations in the budget for both army and navy. "In Brazil," he said, "we are aware that the agents of the Third International can creep into our household by way of doors half-opened by foreigners who have gained illegal entrance, or through gates left carelessly ajar by sleepy citizens. Georgi Dimitroff himself has warned us that the Bolshevik can come like a night burglar or a Trojan horse."

Asked to furnish an outline of the Brazilian program of social reconstruction, President Vargas declared that the payment of a minimum annual wage was the cornerstone of his policy. It was no fault of the worker, he suggested, that employment in the cotton and coffee industry did not extend throughout 12 months of the year. To secure a decent standard of living it was not sufficient that a laborer draw a dollar a day for six months. His expenses, it was argued, were computed on an annual basis and this required that income be considered in the same relationship.

LABOR DISPUTES

With reference to the arbitration of labor disputes the Brazilian leader was even more emphatic. Recalling that his administration had erected machinery for the discussion of difficulties between employers and workers in 1931, he claimed that each succeeding year had witnessed the composition of numerous quarrels without the necessity of either strike or lockout.

"How many countries," Mr. Vargas asked, "can match our record—not a major strike in seven years?" It was his view that this was the direct result of the "Courts of Labor Justice." Brazilians, it may be conceded, have a talent for conciliation and compromise. In recent years they seem successfully to have utilized peaceful means of settling labor disputes.

"Every farmer and city worker," President Vargas added, "has the right to look for protection against the perils and vicissitudes of the future. Security is the watchword of our generation. It is also a passion. To satisfy this aspiration, the government instituted pensions and credit banks." It was his plan to supplement these measures by sickness, unemployment, old age and accident insurance, with special attention to domestic workers.

"The government," he stated, "will help each department of industry and service to organize itself for the sake of its members." Nor would white-collar workers be forgotten. President Vargas pointed out that the Commercial Employes' Institution was already operative in cities and towns among clerks, bookkeepers and salespeople. Two-week holidays with pay was one of the advantages cited.

SOCIAL JUSTICE

"As a result," the Brazilian statesman declared, "family life thrives, while the laborer has a chance to accumulate a tiny nest egg for his children. Social security means social peace. It pays big dividends for the government, for the director of industry and commerce as well as for the general consuming public."

Questioned about transportation problems, Mr. Vargas explained that he was about to initiate a vast program of road, railway and ship construction. He said that lack of means of communication and transport was undoubtedly one of the chief factors in Brazil's slow economic development. The President admitted that it would sometimes take weeks for a letter from the capital to reach remote villages near the headwaters of the Amazon.

Speaking of the motor highway from Rio de Janeiro to Petropolis, he cited it as one example of what could be done to promote automobile traffic. It was interesting to hear that Brazil would continue to be in the market for locomotives, Diesel engines, electrical equipment, freight cars and motorships. This correspondent heard that orders for passenger and freight steamers had already been placed in Italy and Germany. The President estimated that an additional $5,000,000 would be expended for sea transportation alone.

President Vargas was most emphatic in expressing his devotion to the ideals of representative government. "Personal liberty and an equal chance for all citizens to fill administration posts," he declared, "is the essence of democratic institutions. We have no concentration camps, no colored shirts, no tags, labels or badges. The masses of the people have not been militarized; nor is there predominance of one group over another. We preach and practise racial equality."

A REAL DEMOCRACY

Insisting that it would be a mistake to classify Brazil with totalitarian states, the South American statesman reminded this correspondent that his government had warded off an assault from Communist forces of the left in 1931; in 1937 and 1938, he contended, the Vargas administration had been even more successful in repulsing an attack which had been organized by right extremists. "This must make it clear," the President continued, "that we are opposed to both Naziism and

Fascism as well as to Bolshevism. These are all exotic doctrines, so far as Brazil is concerned."

As a sovereign nation, Mr. Vargas pointed out, Brazil looks to herself for protection and policy. Brazilian trade, too, is independent of political ideologies; there is one simple rule: reciprocity.

In concluding the interview the Brazilian President predicted that the day of huge surplus coffee crops had gone forever. "We are taking effective means," he said, "to deal directly with countries which are now receiving coffee from intermediaries. To burn the fruits of the earth is sinful waste. Brazil has terminated that practise. We must learn to utilize our wealth. Potentially Brazil is one of the richest countries in South America, if not in the world. Our problem is to complete a program of social organization that will actualize this richness for the benefit of every citizen. We believe we have made a fair start toward this goal."

CHAPTER XII

DR. OSWALDO ARANHA

A Democratic Foreign Minister

IN AN INTERVIEW granted me by Foreign Minister Oswaldo Aranha at the Itamaraty Palace, Rio de Janeiro, the Brazilian statesman definitely placed his country in the ranks of the democracies at this critical period of world history.

"While we do not seek any quarrel with the totalitarian states," Dr. Aranha explained, "we are inclined by tradition, advantage and sympathy to find a certain common basis for foreign policy in the attitude of our friends in North America. You can say that Brazil is sure to align herself with the democratic axis.

"You can add that Brazil believes that she has adhered strictly to the democratic tradition in her recent governmental changes. By democracy I mean a régime that rests upon the full consent of the governed. Wasn't this Woodrow Wilson's idea? He said 'there is no just government without free consent of the governed.' The Brazilian people whole-heartedly favor the administration of President Vargas and they are eager to cooperate with democratically-minded people throughout the world.

"We are no more apt to imitate the Nazis, or the Fascists, or the Soviets, than we are inclined to substitute German or Italian for our Portuguese language. We can't transform our nature, our tradition, our historic friendships. Foremost among the latter I place the relationship of Brazil with the United States of America. We love and admire the American people. We have confidence in American statesmen such as Ambassador J. H. Jefferson Caffery, the gentleman who now represents your government with admirable tact and skill. We feel that the responsible United States' officials are eager to cooperate with us and to maintain intact the values of mutual respect.

"At the same time," Dr. Aranha warned, "we Brazilians are not tempted to engage in any ideological war. We don't think it helps peace in the world for the democracies to revile dictatorship, or for dictatorship to express its contempt for parliamentarism. Opposition excites opposition. It can easily happen that the authoritarian states will reject and criticize every program, political, social or cultural, simply because it is sponsored by a democratic régime, and vice versa.

"No good purpose is served in becoming blinded to important values that may happen to be found on one side of the barrier or the other. Brazilians, unlike Spaniards, are moderate. They are inclined to seek middle-of-the-road solution. And they greatly dislike disagreements or bloodshed. Democracy, it seems to me, if it is to be true to its name and its nature must seek the *juste milieu*.

"Why can't dictatorships and democracies exist side by side as amicably as did republics and empires one hundred years ago?"

"Brazil has an important obligation to maintain a just balance in foreign policy in view of her geographical position. My country is a neighbor of practically every other South American nation except Chile. Our frontiers are both in the tropics and in the Temperate Zone. Our record in dealing with these different peoples is a narrative of peace and friendship."

Questioned as to whether Brazil's plan to grow her own wheat would jeopardize friendly relations with the Argentine, hitherto the source of much of the Brazilian bread supply, Foreign Minister Aranha replied that his own State, Rio Grande do Sul formerly exported wheat to the Argentine.

"In 1835 and ten succeeding years, Argentina bought grain in Brazil. Even cattle were shipped from Porto Alegre to Buenos Aires. The Argentine authorities understand our program of economic development. They have just sent a military mission to Brazil which is meeting with the most cordial welcome from officers, men and civilians. The ABC countries are friends, if not allies.

"Of course, the United States ranks first in our list of friends. History proves the truth of my assertion. Your country was the first to recognize our independence after the revolt against Portugal. We Brazilians have never forgotten that. At the time of the Civil War President Lincoln said that if the need for mediation should arise Brazil would be the first nation he would welcome in the role of mediator.

"During the Spanish-American War Brazil supplied three warships to the United States. These gunboats fought in the battle of Manila under Admiral Dewey.

Finally during the World War, as soon as the United States saw fit to engage in hostilities, Brazil proclaimed to the world that she could no longer remain neutral. That is a clear picture of our attitude and feeling today. The union of hearts and minds between our nations has never been closer. Indeed, it furnishes a model for imitation. If the same spirit could be evoked in Europe it would provide the era of cooperation and good will so earnestly desired by the masses of the people."

In response to my inquiry as to the best way to consolidate the gains that have been made in relationships between the United States and Brazil Dr. Aranha emphasized the importance of closer cultural relationships.

"There have been all too few American students, professors, professional men and tourists who have seen fit to visit Brazil. We are a country of great potentialities both materially and spiritually. I am sure that American economists, sociologists, health officers and psychologists would make a fine contribution to our national development. Students of anthropology and ethnology will find in Brazil a rich field for research."

Questioned about the influence of the American motion pictures and radio the Foreign minister became positively eloquent. "Some years ago the cinema was doing North America a serious disservice. Foreigners judge Americans by their motion picture stars and motion picture morality. These left something to be desired. It is fortunate that there has been a change of heart in Hollywood. I want to see your people, just, liberal, vital, properly represented.

"In the field of radio," Dr. Aranha continued, "there is room for considerable improvement. Turn on the radio while you are in Rio de Janeiro. You will barely be able to distinguish the voices or the music. Few cultural programs reach us. On the other hand, the German radio stations cultivate the Brazilian public most assiduously. Not only have the German authorities built broadcasting stations that provide perfect reception in the entire extent of Brazil, but they have hired Brazilian announcers who speak our idiom in Brazilian not Portuguese style. On holidays they arrange special programs. The radio experts study our preferences as to programs, music and humor.

"What is the result? The German entertainment and cultural programs are easily the most popular with the Brazilian public. It is the result of careful, systematic planning, quite the opposite of your haphazard American broadcasting to South America. Lately, however, it is a joy to note enormous improvement in the organization and content of American programs.

"If Brazil had received the consideration and co-operation which has been accorded to Mexico, she would be in a much stronger position internally and internationally. I am hopeful that the inauguration of new, fast steamship service between New York and the eastern coast of South America will awaken North America to a realization of what good friends your people have in all classes of the Brazilian population."

CHAPTER XIII

DR. OSWALDO ARANHA

Brazilian-American Catholic Cooperation

MY SECOND interview with Dr. Oswaldo Aranha, Foreign Minister of Brazil, also took place in the famous Itamaraty Palace in Rio de Janeiro. Dr. Aranha, thanks to horseback riding and tennis, retains a youthful figure and immense vitality. This physical fitness is reflected in his mental processes. Unlike most Foreign Secretaries he answers questions directly, adequately. His democratic principles are well known. In fact, it is an open secret in Washington that his presence in the Brazilian Cabinet more than any other single factor allayed the suspicion that the great South American Federation was moving into the orbit of totalitarian States.

As Ambassador of Brazil to the United States, Dr. Aranha had won golden opinions for his diplomatic abilities as well as for his sincere adherence to liberal political views. Without a Foreign Minister of this type it is doubtful whether the régime of President Getulio Vargas would have survived the storm of adverse criticism which greeted the *coup d'état* of November 10, 1937. Conversations with Secretary Aranha convinced

100

me that confidence in his democratic convictions was not misplaced.

My first question concerned the extent and intensity of Fascist and Nazi influence in Brazil. The Foreign Minister was amazingly frank.

"Everybody in Brazil knows how eager Germany and Italy are to secure our friendship," he declared. "The Germans in particular have erected powerful radio stations in order to broadcast their programs directly to the people of this country. They have taken pains to hire announcers who speak Brazilian Portuguese; they excogitate programs that flatter the *amour-propre* of the Brazilians. On our national holidays, for example, the Berlin station thrills the public with the Brazilian patriotic songs. Speeches are delivered showing an intimate knowledge of Brazil's history, traditions and culture. The commercial element in the programs is either minimized or utterly eliminated. This contributes to the entertainment value of the broadcasts."

Dr. Aranha insisted that the extent of Nazi or Fascist influence in Brazil had been exaggerated in the American press. He did not deny that strenuous efforts had been made to create good will for foreign ideologies (including Marxism) in Brazil, but he deplored the impression that Brazil had gone over to totalitarianism.

"The Government of President Getulio Vargas," he said, "is distinctively Brazilian without any tincture of foreign 'isms.' Do you think I would have accepted office in an administration that either owed its origin to or submitted to dictation from a European nation? We don't intend to transfer any ideological war to the South American continent.

"The *Integralista*, or Green Shirt movement, was the work of a few irresponsible boys. You can see how thoroughly Getulio Vargas outlawed the movement. If any European governments subsidized this group it has been a poor investment. The leaders are either in jail or in hiding. President Vargas did not even think it necessary to mete out summary capital punishment to the assassins who attempted to murder him in the Executive Mansion in the spring of 1938. Do you think Mussolini or Hitler would deal with high treason in this spirit? We do not intend to invent any martyrs for those who may happen to differ with us in the domain of politics.

"President Vargas will submit his new constitution to a plebiscite. The people will decide what reforms are needed to weld our immense territory and huge population into a homogeneous unit. In the new constitution guarantees of liberty of speech, liberty of the press, liberty of peaceful assembly and liberty of conscience will be conspicuous. There is nothing totalitarian about the program."

The Foreign Minister then alluded to the public support expressed for the new regime by the Archbishop of Rio de Janeiro, His Eminence, Don Sebastian Cardinal Leme.

"Do you suppose," he asked, "that this approval from the highest ecclesiastical authority in Brazil would have been vouchsafed, unless the Cardinal Archbishop were persuaded that fundamental liberties would remain intact?"

We had now been speaking for almost a solid hour. The Secretary, thoroughly absorbed by his subject, became more cordial, revealing. Throwing aside the ordinary conventions imposed by diplomatic protocol he spoke freely, without restraint or reserve.

"Isn't there a special role for the Catholics of North America in the campaign to bring about closer cultural cooperation between the people of the United States and Brazil?" he inquired. "I am thinking particularly of the laity in the two countries. There are numerous Catholic societies in North America that have their counterparts in Brazil. While I was in Washington I was often edified and impressed by the work of the lay leaders in the Knights of Columbus, The Holy Name Society, the Sodality of the Blessed Virgin, the Catholic Daughters of America and the International Federation of Catholic Alumnae. Why should not the officers of these groups do more to promote closer spiritual relationship with their fellow Christians in Brazil?"

With animation of gesture and eloquence of voice Dr. Aranha continued to emphasize what he called the appropriateness and the utility of more frequent, intimate relationships between the Catholics of Brazil and those of the United States. It was his view that Brazilian Catholics would gain much from the example of lay organizations in the United States, while North American Catholics, as well as Christians throughout the world, could derive much fruit from a study of Brazil's efforts to combat Communism and to inaugurate a system of social justice that would give practical effect to the principles contained in the Papal Encyclicals.

"Brazilians," Foreign Minister Aranha declared, "have a tremendous admiration for the achievements of the North American people." They believe, he said, that North Americans "have a good sense of life and its best values," and for this reason, he added, it was one of his most fervent desires "to bring a large number of North Americans into personal contact" with leading Brazilian citizens, institutions and scientific organizations. He added that the Catholic Church in North America, "which has attained such a position of respect and influence should take the initiative in this matter."

Citing the campaign of President Vargas against Communism, which he said dealt Marxism one of its most crushing blows in the New World, Dr. Aranha declared that United States Catholics "should find material for study, if not imitation, in the success which we Brazilians have had in outwitting the Soviets."

When I inquired as to the possibility of Brazil establishing formal diplomatic relations with the Soviet Union, I was assured emphatically that "no such project would be entertained by the present government."

At the same time, the Foreign Secretary emphasized that more than negative measures were envisaged for the war against radical, subversive agitators. Brazil's attempt under its new Constitution to apply at least in broad outline some of the principles of the social Encyclicals of Pius XI is another reason why Catholics should take a special interest in Brazil, he said. "Students of social reconstruction," he asserted, "agree that these principles offer substantial hope for the solution of our most acute problems of housing, unemployment, surplus production, suitable living standards, and a comprehensive program of health and recreation for the general public.

"The cooperation and sympathetic interest of American Christian sociologists would become a powerful lever in the application of our constitutional program. The corporative system (or organization of vocational bodies) is succeeding in Portugal, a nation with which we have considerable racial and cultural affinity. Our President is planning a visit to Portugal in order to gain the latest information of the development of this movement."

To be frank, this writer saw little or no evidence of "occupational bodies" in Brazil. The walls were still plastered with colored posters advertising the virtues of the "corporative" system, but beyond these paper notices there was nothing to show that workers and employers had even heard the outline of the Papal program, except in the workingmen circles that have been organized under the direction of the Catholic Hierarchy.

That there is ample scope for a campaign to apply the *Rerum Novarum* and *Quadragesimo Anno* however, is clear from the fact that skilled laborers in Rio de Janeiro usually do not receive a daily wage in excess of twenty milreis, which would be less than one dollar in American money. Unskilled workers, of course, do not get more than half a dollar a day for their services, while domestic servants (or household assistants) are recompensed by food, lodging, and a tiny stipend of a few dollars a month. In this connection, it must be mentioned that living expenses do not absorb as much of the worker's income as would corresponding expenditures in the United States. No one starves or freezes to death in Brazil.

As our interview drew to a close Dr. Aranha startled me by the remark that "Brazil is the largest Catholic nation in the world as well as the country with the largest percentage of Catholics in the total population.

"Is not that fact in itself sufficient to elicit the friendly attention of your 21,000,000 Catholics who are the most numerous religious group in the Western Hemisphere north of the Equator?" he asked.

With obvious enthusiasm the Foreign Minister recommended exchange scholarships in American and Brazilian universities, stating that exchange professorships on the scale of what is being done between the United States and Europe would be a helpful feature in the development of better cultural relationships between Brazilian and United States Catholics.

This correspondent knows that the policy of cultured cooperation has not been neglected by educators who owe no allegiance to Catholicism. There are a number of North Americans teaching in the colleges and universities of Brazil. The United States intellectual influence is strongly felt both in Rio de Janeiro, the capital of the Federation, and in Sao Paulo, capital of the most powerful Brazilian State. According to Arthur Ramos, professor of social psychology in the University of the Federal District, "North American sociology tends more and more to dominate the active social centres of Brazil. The *grande animador* is Delgado de Carvalho, whose books bristle with the names of Lester Ward, Giddings, Park Burgess, Cooley, Ross and Ellwood."

This gave point to the Foreign Minister's final suggestion:

"We welcome lay interest and lay participation in the program of social development which is getting under way in Brazil," he said. "Perhaps it may be possible for some of the North American organizations to hold their conferences or conventions in Rio de Janeiro, or Sao Paulo. Naturally, our men in public life would welcome the International Eucharistic Congress to our capital. Furthermore, our professional men and women seek the opportunity to discuss common problems with Catholic doctors, surgeons, lawyers, engineers, artists, dentists, journalists and university professors.

"Our closest ties are still with the people of the United States of America and I am persuaded that the Catholic Church in your country, with its splendid tradition of patriotism and educational service which I have witnessed at first-hand, can make a most valuable contribution to a better undertstanding of Brazil in North America."

CHAPTER XIV

GENERAL EDOUARD De CASTELNAU

The Chief of French Catholic Action

IN THE early spring of 1916, the French armies on the Western Front were beginning to crumble before the German attack at Verdun. The officers forming the entourage of Marshal Joseph Jacques Joffre, the Commander-in-Chief, engrossed with plans for a gigantic offensive of their own, were not moved, much less disturbed. The Verdun offensive, they explained to their chief, was only a feint. The main blow would be launched on the opposite front. But on the night of February 24, reports became so alarming that General Edouard De Curieres De Castelnau, in the words of Captain Liddell Hart, "insisted that one of the *aides-de-camp* should knock on Joffre's bedroom door, regularly locked at ten o'clock to shut out all disturbers of his sleep."

Wide-eyed the Commander-in-Chief listened to hurried warnings, and before the midnight interview was ended, he had given Castelnau authority to travel through the night to Verdun with "full powers" to deal with the situation. A reinforcement of two army corps was thrown into the breach, arriving in time to stiffen

108

"a frail and cracking line." Further measures of defense were entrusted to General Henri Phillipe Pétain, and Castelnau, the alert Chief of Staff, had once more done his part to save his country from her external enemies.

There is an unmistakable resemblance between Castelnau's action on this occasion and his singuarly opportune defense of France from her internal enemies after the war. In 1924, the *Bloc National* disintegrated and power passed into the hands of the huge *Cartel de Gauches*. Edouard Herriot, the Prime Minister, was unblushing in his hostility to the Church and to Catholic institutions. No time was wasted in preliminary skirmishing. In the interests of "moral peace," he announced, the French Embassy to the Vatican was to be suppressed, the laws regarding religious congregations were to be "applied," and the legislative differences between Alsace Lorraine (where Catholic rights in education were guaranteed) and the rest of France were to be obliterated. This program, it was well known had been drawn up in the "caves" of the Grand Orient, and Herriot, in making the announcement to the French Chamber, was merely acting as the mouthpiece of continental Freemasonry. Couched in elegant phraseology the government formulas were intended to pronounce a valedictory over the *Union Sacrée,* which had served France so well in her hour of need. Another enemy had advanced on a second Verdun.

The emphatic "No!" uttered by the loyal citizens of Alsace and Lorraine, was the signal for Catholic resistance. It was strengthened by the celebrated letter of Père Paul Doncoeur, whose words, *Nous ne partirons pas,* eloquently expressed the courage and patriotism of his brother priests and Religious. Was it merely a coincidence that "We will not go" seemed to echo the rallying cry at Verdun, "They shall not pass?" Here and there a meeting was held by the League for the Defence of Religious Rights. At this unexpected show of opposition the Masonic offensive halted discreetly, lost momentum, and hovered about, rather than assailed its object. It was a scene of doubt and confusion.

The Catholics, too, were wavering. As had happened so often in the past, differences of social outlook and divisions along political lines threatened to continue a source of fatal weakness. Many groups consulted apart, assuming the appearance and policy of factions. It seemed inevitable that the centers of Catholic action, powerful as they were in the aggregate, would once more cancel each other out.

At this critical moment, when the enemy was mobilizing for a renewed offensive, a leader emerged whose name and character welded together the scattered forces of the Catholic reaction. It was the hero of Verdun, whose keen, strategic eyes surveyed the situation as unerringly as they had recognized the military importance of that semicircle of hills that guarded Fort Douaumont. A born leader of men, he neither courted nor shrank from responsibility. His first speech at Rodez in the prefecture of Rouergue rang throughout France. Responding to the popular approval, the Commission of Cardinals and Archbishops entrusted to M. le général Castelnau the task of realizing a nation-wide Catholic union.

As soon as General Castelnau was installed in the central office at Paris, support poured in from all sides.

Encouragement, counsel, and help were furnished by the entire French episcopate. Diocesan committees were formed. In November, 1924, thirty-one such well-knit groups had been increased to eighty-six, representing every diocese. Mass meetings were held in the large centers. Their success had been assured by careful preparation in the parish assemblies.

Castelnau was everywhere that winter. Like a general hastening from point to point on the battlefield, he scattered encouragement, praise, advice, and exhortation. The Catholic ranks closed; columns formed; words of command were followed by uniform action. From January, 1925, to September, 1926, no less than 1,832,000 men participated in meetings of what was now the National Catholic Federation of France.

The Herriot government was stupefied. Reports from the various prefectures left no doubt as to the national character of the organization and the determined convictions of its adherents. The Socialists, Communists, atheists, and hierophants of the Grant Orient, accustomed to trample Catholic rights in the dust, found they had to reckon with a new Christian crusade, a virile Federation, which marched to the chant of the ancient and eternal *Credo*. The anti-Catholic program was relinquished. The new national Catholic group had attained its first objective—the warding off of a dangerous offensive.

The Herriot Government then signed its own death warrant by a reckless financial policy, which launched the French franc on the dizzy whirlpool of inflation. Extravagant expenditure, continued budget deficits, and currency depreciation led to one Cabinet crisis after another until the agony was relieved by the Ramon Poincaré Government of 1926.

In the meantime the Catholics consolidated their forces and, with the blessing of the Holy Father, Pius XI, prepared a positive, constructive program of Catholic action. First and foremost, it was stated, that French Catholics could not accept a status of diminished or detruncated citizenship. If citizens had the right of association, why should this be denied to French citizens who happened to be religious? If citizens had the right to choose a school for their children, the corollary was obvious that they should not on that account be penalized by double taxation.

Maintenance of Catholic rights in education in restored provinces was indicated as the only course compatible with solemn promises made to the inhabitants of Alsace and Lorraine. Catholics could not tolerate, in exchange for services rendered, the continued spoliation and persecution of the Church. Diocesan associations, legally established, were entitled to receive legacies, donations, subventions, and endowments proper to their foundation and social purpose. The reestablishment of the Embassy to the Vatican was taken for granted.

Most interesting were the far-sighted provisions in the Catholic program for what was called a sound *politique familiale*. This aimed to promote the health, morals, and growth of the French family, urging a family wage, proper rest, recreation, social insurance, and means to allot the fundamental group of society a definite place in public life. These points bore fruit in subsequent social legislation.

In a country of ardent political passions it was emphasized that the National Catholic Federation had a distinctively spiritual object, that it was outside of and above all political parties, and that it sought above all the supernatural perfection of souls. At the same time the organization felt it was rendering a service to the temporal welfare of the state in restoring Christ in the family, the school, and society. In short, its ideal was Catholic Action according to the mind of Pius XI, and its grand General Castelnau, working in the closest collaboration with the Bishops, priests, and people, was not ineptly styled the "Minister of Catholic Action."

The years, 1926-28, therefore, were years of public education. The textbooks, we may say, were the great Encyclicals of Leo XIII, Pius X, Benedict XV, and Pius XI. Meetings, parochial and diocesan, were unceasing and national aims were coordinated in general assemblies which represented as a rule seventy-five to eighty of the eighty-six dioceses in France. A whole new press was created whose principal organs, the *Credo,* the *Point de direction,* and the *Correspondance Hebdomadaire* had a total circulation of four and a half millions a year.

The fruits of this campaign of public education were shown in the elections of 1928. While carefully refraining from any partisan political activity, the Catholic committees in each district proposed a definite set of questions (respecting Catholic rights) to the candidates. Catholic support was promised only to those who accepted these engagements. Many non-Catholic Deputies recognized the justice of the Catholic claims and agreed to support them in the Chamber. The result was that as many as 277 members were elected either by the Catholics or with Catholic cooperation. This figure represented forty-four per cent of the Chamber. For an initial effort this was not discouraging.

The chief lesson of the movement, however, was the importance of the ballot as an instrument of justice. It had long been the opinion in Catholic circles that there was no such thing as "good elections." The 277 Deputies, who would not have been elected without Catholic help, were a shock and a stimulus to electoral apathy. Here was hope for representative government. Politicians do yield to constant moral pressure. Even a radical or Masonic deputy, it was found, would not make sport of the convictions of a third or a fourth of his constituency, provided the latter was organized and active.

After all, the good-natured politicians began to conclude, religious men and women should be free to live as they choose; the curés, however dull a lot in general, in particular districts (their own) were not as bad as in others; they gave excellent instruction to children, while the nuns certainly seemed to be skilful nurses and devoted helpers of the old, the feeble, and the poor. What a difference of outlook a few votes made! The Catholics repeated the lesson to themselves: "It is necessary to organize and exact promises, where fundamental human rights are at stake."

Needless to say, the new Chamber did not talk about "applying the laws about the religious congregations." In fact, it was proposed to revise the so-called "intangible laws." In April, 1929, the Deputies voted to legalize the return of nine missionary congregations. Aiming as it did to extend French political influence, this measure was a limited and narrowly nationalistic approach to the problem.

The principle of religious freedom was not involved. For this reason the National Catholic Federation refused to undertake *une belle agitation* to pass the measure. The leaders were unwilling to compromise themselves for the future by acquiescing in the view that the foreign missionaries were agents of French culture rather than ambassadors of Christ. Consequently, the modified motion that received the approval of the Chamber was even less liberal and by no means satisfied legitimate Catholic aspirations. Nevertheless all the Religious Orders returned to France. Although still lacking formal legal sanction, they were established on the basis of a "statute of fact," guaranteed by the presence of the National Catholic Federation.

From 1928 to 1932, the work of the Federation has continued on the lines marked out by General Castelnau, the President, and his able committees. On February 8, 1928, they demanded an inquiry on social insurance and supported the ensuing legislation through the Chamber.

In the municipal elections of 1929, Catholics were returned in larger numbers to the town councils. The importance of what we Americans would call "precinct organization" came to be better understood. All energies were being directed to secure a better representation of Catholic rights in the Chamber of Deputies to be elected in the spring of 1932. In short, Catholic Action in France, far from remaining the privilege of a small élite, had assumed the proportions of a mass movement of militant Christians.

Each year the Federation made a solemn pilgrimage to the Basilica of the Sacred Heart at Montmartre, where General De Castelnau renewed the consecration of the movement to the Sacred Heart of Jesus. In that same Basilica a few years ago, this devoted soldier of Christ received on his eightieth birthday the Grand Cross of the Order of St. Gregory the Great. The honor was conferred by Cardinal Verdier, Archbishop of Paris, in the name of His Holiness Pius XI. Truly the work of Monsieur le général had been blessed by God and men. It may confidently be assumed that the blessing operative under the hard adverse circumstances will be a pledge and a promise of greater achievements for God and country in happier days.

(NOTE: These facts were gathered in a personal interview with General De Castelnau at the headquarters of the National Catholic Federation in Paris.)

CHAPTER XV

JOSEPH MOTTA

President of Switzerland

As a Catholic statesman, President Joseph Motta of Switzerland deserved more than passing notice. He first took office as President of the Swiss Confederation when Europe was in the throes of the World War and maintained the armed neutrality of his country, in spite of tremendous pressure brought to bear on him to favor one side or the other. Afterwards, in the worldwide effort to liquidate the effects of the War, he played a leading part on the European scene, serving his fellow citizens five times as head of the Swiss Federal Council.

Motta was endowed with extraordinary natural powers. As a boy, he had shown unusual love of books and study. His gifts of eloquence were unmistakable. After preliminary studies in his native canton of Ticino, he was sent to the gymnasium of Ascona and then to the College of St. Michel at Fribourg. It was at the Catholic University of Fribourg that he mastered philosophy and letters, besides adding French and German to a knowledge of Italian, his mother tongue.

On this triple foundation he was able to build the admirable culture, which revealed itself in his discourses,

117

where citations from Dante and Goethe side by side with passages from the great French authors went to the end of his life. The *Divina Commedia* remained his book of predilection, while his habit of reading and speaking the three languages had been perfected by daily exercise. Small wonder that such a brilliant student should crown his law courses at Munich and Heidelberg by the Doctorate won *summa cum laude*.

His native village was Airolo, at the foot of St. Gothard, where his family had lived for generations and where his father had combined two functions: that of innkeeper and postal concessionary. Thither the youthful advocate returned, hoping to win a modest income at the bar. His mother, who had been left a widow at an early age, had made great sacrifices to give her boy the opportunities for study his talents required and Joseph Motta was eager to relieve what had already become an almost intolerable burden. In a very true sense he owed everything to his mother, as he himself testified:

"I can never be too grateful to my mother, who, left a widow when I was still a child, engraved on my heart the idea of obligation, teaching me that duty must dominate all interests, all instincts of selfishness, all preoccupations, and that the rule of duty was what man ought to take for a guide in all the journeys and storms of life."

This mother was sprung from the stock of the canton of Uri, at once the cradle of Swiss liberty and a stronghold of the Catholic Faith. Mme. Motta's influence on her son was decisive. Both energetic and intelligent, a type of the valiant woman of Holy Scripture, she preserved an ascendancy over Joseph Motta which guided him through the early stages of his career.

He needed every bit of advice and counsel, because, although only twenty-five years of age, he had already been tempted by the demon of politics. In the canton of Ticino, the party struggle raged as furiously as years before in the ancient Italian communes. The *Conservateurs-populaires* (for the most part Catholics) were just beginning to dispute the power and influence of the radicals, noted for their violent anti-clerical traditions. Motta, fervent Catholic that he was, fought in the ranks of the conservative group and soon won a place of undisputed leadership.

In 1894, he took his first step toward national prominence by securing election on the great Council of the Canton of Ticino. From that moment his ascent was rapid. Four years later found him on the national Council, where he continued to represent the *Conservateurs-populaires* until 1911. In that year and by a record vote, he entered the supreme Federal Council as chief of the Department of Finance. His first thought on this occasion was characteristic: he dispatched two telegrams, one to his mother, the other to his wife. Obviously, he did not consider his success apart from the sources of his strength and virtue.

It is important to note that the Swiss Federal Council is the executive organ of Government. The seven members which comprise it do not represent their party, but their region. The wise purpose of this provision is to maintain a certain equilibrium among the three elements —German, French, and Italian—which make up the country. Although elected by the General Assembly, the

Federal Councilors are not responsible to it, and, as a result, the Assembly has no authority to overthrow them. Otherwise, their position is equivalent to that of Cabinet Ministers, and, since they are eligible for re-election, they are usually maintained in office as long as age, infirmity, or exceptional circumstances permit. In this way, the members of the Federal Council, like the Sea Lords in the British Admiralty, are permanent functionaries or supreme administrative chiefs, who assure great stability to government and considerable continuity to matters of high policy.

It is in this charmed circle that M. Motta served for thirty years: nine years as head of the Department of Finance and nineteen years in the more congenial field of Foreign Affairs. Five times, in 1915, 1920, 1927, 1932, and 1937, he was called upon to head this chosen group as President of the Confederation. With characteristic modesty, President Motta explained to me that this office rotated by seniority and merely means he was *primus inter pares,* the first among equals. But it is worthy of note that he was the first representative of the Italian element in Switzerland to occupy the exalted chair of chief magistrate.

Even as President he continued to grapple with the routine work of his department. He never missed a day at his desk, giving a striking example of devotion to duty to his subordinates. He arrived at his office at eight o'clock in the morning, remained there as a rule until one o'clock and finished off the day from two to seven. In case there was a residue of work, something not at all unusual, he put the documents under his arm and took them home for completion after dinner. Nevertheless, he found time to read the contemporary reviews in French, German, Italian, and English, and refreshed his soul from day to day with copious draughts from the great classic literatures.

As head of the Department of Foreign Policy, he has played a leading role in the development of the League of Nations. He sincerely believed in the possibilities of the Geneva institution and never missed an opportunity to further its influence. He was named Honorary President of the First Session of the League Assembly (1920) and solemnly opened its initial session. Curiously enough, his début as an orator in that gathering of the nations pitted him against the atheist René Viviani and the decline of the latter in national and international politics dated from his defeat at the hands of the sturdy Swiss patriot. M. Motta stood upon the principle of the League's universality; nor in subsequent debates had he ever swerved from that position. Year after year, Switzerland sent him as her chief delegate to Geneva and the League utilized his talents on some of its most important commissions. In 1924, he was elected President of the Assembly, while later he was Honorary President of the World Conference for the Limitation and Reduction of Armaments. Great Swiss patriot that he was, he did not hesitate to recognize the superior claims of humanity and Christian brotherhood.

Most enlightening in this connection were President Motta's own words: "To oppose Latins and Germans, to make of them irreconcilable enemies, is not only to accomplish an evil deed, but it is also and most especially, to lay violent hands on the rights of Christian civilization." This was the language of a Christian leader, who

looked beyond race, nationality, and blood, to the supernatural bonds of God-made-man. The Swiss statesman
illustrated that a Catholic is the best internationalist.

Important as are President Motta's contributions to
national security and world peace, it is pleasant to record
that his family life was perhaps the most inspiring aspect
of his career. Happily married to a Catholic girl of his
native canton, he was blessed with a famliy of ten
children. One of the daughters entered religion and the
others enjoy the advantages of Catholic education and
training. All are tenderly devoted to the Holy Mass, and
the parish priest of Airolo boasted no more faithful,
humble parishioners than those of the Motta household.
In fine, M. Motta lived his Faith. He was what the
French call *un Catholique croyant et pratiquant*, a
Catholic, who really believes and practices his belief.

At the same time, President Motta was scrupulously
correct in his demeanor as head of the Swiss Federation.
Although he visited Rome, for example, he had not felt
free to pay his respects to the Sovereign Pontiff, because
he feared he might compromise both the Holy Father
and his own situation as President of a country where
different religions are freely practised. This attitude is
apparently understood in Rome, inasmuch as Monsignor
Luigi Maglione, the Apostolic Nuncio at Paris, reported
that Pius XI entertained the highest esteem for M.
Motta, who, on his side, always openly declared his
absolute submission to the Church, adding that the
desires of the Holy Father were sacred in his eyes.

In a beautiful family fête, surrounded by his wife and
ten children, it was this writer's privilege to see President
Motta celebrate his sixtieth birthday anniversary. He

did not look bowed down by years. In fact, he appeared in the full possession of his best physical vigor, if not of complete youthfulness. Very erect in his meager inches, extremely alert and attentive, he seemed to retain something of the freshness of the soil of his native Ticino. His eyes, the eyes of Italy, were full of life and fire, luminous, ardent, friendly. Smiling, he was irresistible. Conciliation and a temperament endowed for diplomacy were writ large on that calm, regular countenance. His complexion was ruddy and clear, the result of winters in Berne and summers on the southern slope of the Alps. The hair, abundant, short-cropped, gray, formed a silver frame for his handsome, high forehead. Closing my eyes for a moment, I could picture him in another gathering, addressing a congress of Swiss Catholic students:

"Love ideas. That is the profound meaning I would attach to the words of your motto: *Scientia.* It is not an individual slavery to which Christ called humanity, but to the superior liberty of the children of light . . . Love ideas and share boldly in that intellectual labor which tends to liberate us from the materialistic doctrines imported from alien lands and so contrary to our national genius."

Could there, asked the special correspondent of the *Revue des Deux Mondes,* have been "nobler language or an admonition more opportune?"

CHAPTER XVI

FRANCISCO FRANCO

The Marshal Foch of Christian Spain

LIKE MOST favorites of destiny, Generalissimo Francisco Franco owes much to his Mother. Pilar Bahamonde shaped the life of her son, the second of five children, in two important respects: religion and a sense of social justice. She taught by deeds rather than by words. She was religious and she was just.

When Ramón Franco, the fourth child of the family, was enjoying his brief hour of glorious triumph after a record-breaking air flight to South America, the applauding multitude sought the Señora Franco y Bahamonde. Where was she found? Neither in the public square nor in the city hall of El Ferrol, Franco's native place, but in the church for the solemn chanting of a *Te Deum* of thanksgiving. As General Franco's most recent biographer, Joaquin Arrarás, puts it, she "was satisfied to give thanks to Heaven during long hours of prayer which she spent in the solitude of the churches of El Ferrol."*

*Joaquin Arrarás *Francisco Franco*, p. 6. Translated by J. Manuel Espinosa, Ph.D. Milwaukee—The Bruce Publishing Company (1938).

124

While praise resounded on every side, inspired by the brave exploit of her son, Pilar Bahamonde escaped from celebrations and receptions in order to maintain her teaching schedule in the Workers' Night School, where she elucidated the social principles of Leo XIII and Pius XI. Throughout the years of dictatorship, wars in Morocco and political agitation, this Christian matron continued to instruct the miners, farmers, mechanics, artisans, ship-carpenters, wool-workers and domestic servants of her native province of Galicia in their right to a family wage, a just price for agricultural products and all that we now grandly describe as social security. Her boy Francisco had become the youngest general in the army; his brother, Ramón, had piloted the airplane, PLUS ULTRA, from Spain to Pernambuco; she herself remained true to the apostolate of social justice she had chosen as her avocation. Both virtues, as a result, were planted in the heart of her talented son.

The birth of Francisco Franco is on record in the register of the military parish of San Francisco, El Ferrol, Galicia. Born on the fourth of December, 1892, he was not baptized until the seventeenth of that month. He was brought into the world at "one half hour midnight on the fourth day of that month, and baptized with the names of Francisco, Paulino, Hermenegildo, and Teodulo; the son of the naval paymaster Nicolas Franco and Pilar Bahamonde."

Francisco's early education was obtained in The School of the Sacred Heart, conducted by a splendid priest of El Ferrol named Marcos Vazquez. True to the tradition of his family, Franco then entered the Naval

School in the same city, pursuing a course that led to the Bachelor of Arts degree. The next step, natural to one whose ancestors numbered Admirals and Vice-Admirals of the Fleet, would have been an examination for entrance to the national Naval Academy.

This is where America first intervened in the future Generalissimo's career. The Spanish fleet was at the bottom of the sea around Santiago, Cuba, and Manila, the Philippine Islands.

The youthful Franco had to content himself with a candidacy for the Toledo Military Academy, which he entered on August 29, 1907. Three years later, he was graduated with honors and commissioned as second lieutenant, July 13, 1910. He was an officer of the King.

The next year witnessed defeat and disaster in Morocco. The military situation in this Spanish colonial possession was both a tragedy and a humiliation. Few military men coveted a post in that poverty-stricken, unhappy land, the devourer of warriors. But defeat and despair did not deter Lieutenant Franco. He volunteered and was dispatched to Melilla. In his eyes the mission signified action, war, patriotic service.

In the late Spring of 1912 (May 14), Colonel Berenguer, commanding a detachment of Regulars, met the enemy in the vicinity of Yadumen.

A squadron of cavalry, far in the vanguard, attracted the attention of Colonel Berenguer. "That section is advancing very well," was his admiring exclamation.

"That section," he was told, "is led by Franco."

Again and again this observation is to be repeated: "Franco led the shock troops; the enemy is retreating."

Wounds, decorations, promotions, posts of honor and

danger followed in rapid succession. One of the first was the Cross of Maria Cristina. He was affectionately styled "the little Major." Wherever he rode or walked, he was singled out for admiring glances and whispered comment: "He is just a boy . . . So serious, so proud, and so young!" More than one began to feel that here was a man of destiny.

On April 28, 1920, the Ministers of the Royal Government created what was speedily to become the famous FOREIGN LEGION. Its organizer and first commander was Lieutenant-Colonel Milan Astray. The latter's first choice for a colleague in this enterprise was Francisco Franco. A few months later, Franco was with the nucleus of the Legion at Algeciras. "Long live Spain!" and "Long live the Legion!" were soon to become familiar watchwords in the Peninsula and in Morocco.

The Spanish Legion had its first scorching baptism of fire at Melilla in 1921. The army had been defeated; the city was defenseless; panic settled over the civilian population. In the rescue effort, led by the Legion, Milan Astray fell wounded. His subordinate, Franco, shouting "Forward!" swept through the enemy to liberate Melilla. The operation had been effected with a minimum number of casualties.

At the conclusion of the campaign General Berenguer made his report. It was eloquent in its simplicity:

"This important event passed completely unnoticed in Spain, where it was received coldly, few being aware of its significance, which was nothing less than the consummation of our objectives in the territory of Melilla and the final point of advance."

To Major Franco, for his part in this happy result, was awarded the Military Medal, an honor second only to that conferred by the Cross of San Fernando.

Valenzuela was now the commander of the Legion (1921-23). On the evening of an important mission he broke into the tent of the chaplain of the regiment.

"Father, I should like to have you hear my confession," he stated calmly, "because in a few hours I am going to die."

The next day, with bullets in head and chest, he fell. The Legion was left without a leader. Whereupon the head of the State declared:

"There is no one who surpasses Franco. He is the unanimous choice."

The Major was promoted to the rank of Lieutenant-Colonel and established as commander of the Spanish Legion. This, the first promotion in the army for two years, was the seal of approval for courage, the supreme law of the Legion.

At this point, it is necessary to emphasize that Francisco Franco, although essentially a man of camps, bivouacs, battle-fields and forced marches, is none the less a compassionate Christian, whose heart is filled with love and sympathy both for his own soldiers and the enemy against whom he is obliged to fight.

There is nothing callous, brutal or inhuman in his attitude toward his troops. Indeed, his victory in Spain was the fruit of confidence among the rank and file of every unit in his army that not a single life would be uselessly exposed. Unlike General Byng, the British chieftain in the World War, who led his men to the butcheries of Paeschendale and Ypres, Francisco Franco never ordered an offensive until the path had been cleared by adequate artillery and aerial preparation. The civilian populations were warned; neutral commissions were recommended to supervise the evacuation of cities that were to be the objectives of a military campaign; every opportunity was afforded for honorable capitulation or surrender. Then, and only then, were the battalions of death told to hold themselves ready to go over the top.

On March 18, 1938, in my radio speech over the Columbia Broadcasting System national network, I placed upon Indalecio Prieto, ex-Minister of National Defense in the Barcelona Government, chief responsibility for the tragic loss of life which ensued upon the bombing of Barcelona and Valencia. That charge may be reiterated with the added condemnation of the Barcelona Cabinet itself. The latter, after the "glorious retreat" from Teruel, exposing as it did the helpless condition of Barcelona after the short-sighted Prieto had stripped the coast-line of protective planes, demanded the immediate, unconditional resignation of the misnamed Minister of Public Defense. The civilian populations of Seville and Salamanca, who were also from time to time the intended victims of Russian air raids, did not enter any such accusation against the true defender of the Spanish people, Generalissimo Franco, Christian and patriot.

It is related by Franco's biographer, and has been a matter of personal observation on my own part, that General Franco, as far as humanly possible, spared both civilians and soldiers the horrors of war. In camp he visited the bed-side of wounded comrades; he was anxious about an outbreak of illness or fever; he was concerned about the extremes of nervous fatigue, shell-shock and spiritual crisis which inevitably accompany the clang of arms. When military men, crippled in soul or body, came to the Generalissimo for comfort, they were greeted like brothers, buoyed up by his superior morale, heartened by his courageous optimism, fired by his enthusiasm for a victorious cause.

In one of the panoramic meditations of St. Ignatius Loyola, entitled "The Kingdom of Christ," a human leader is portrayed as a kingly, knightly figure, willing to share all hardships, dangers and sacrifices with his followers. That figure is an image of General Franco, the Marshal Foch of Christian Spain. The snow of the African mountains and the tropical heat of the desert sun found him in the front ranks of his comrades. Their risks, wounds, privations, were very part of his career. He shrank from no extreme of suffering that he had ordained in the orders of the day for his men. As a result, they surged with him through a breach in the enemy lines, never stopping until under his direction and by reason of his skill they bathed their tired, dusty bodies in the clear, blue waters of the Mediterranean!

Has it been forgotten how the heroes of the Alcazar, Toledo, nourishing themselves on horse-flesh and brown bread, held out when they received the radio flash from the coast that the legions of Franco were on their way? They retained fresh in their memory the story of another rescue, this time in Spanish Morocco, when Lieutenant Topete, besieged by Arabs at Tifarauin, deciphered the message from his commander-in-chief: "Hold out for a few more hours. Franco is coming to your rescue."

"If Franco is coming," the sun-mirror of Tifarauin flashed back, "we shall hold out. *Viva España!*"

Just as at Teruel, Franco, moving forward to the theatre of war, carried out meticulous personal examinations of the topography, the terrain, the roads, mountains and valleys, through which his divisions were to cut their way. In this connection, the judgment of General Fernandez Perez is interesting:

"Despite his youth, he has a cool, calm mind, is calculating in his decisions, and is calm in action, combining admirably these qualities . . . which lead him to examine operations from dangerous positions in order to base his decisions on personal observations . . ."

Unlike Napoleon, Franco is an Alpine climber, leaving no foothold uncertain, reinforcing his lines of communication until free from the strongest possible counter-attack.

If the Generalissimo has faults, and no one familiar with human nature would try to represent him as a paragon of military virtue, he is somewhat inclined to an excess of caution, reflecting his scrupulous respect for the lives and safety of his soldiers, as well as to a slightly exaggerated sense of the need of detailed preparation. This was one factor in the success of the International Brigades in repelling the Nationalist attacks upon Madrid, the apparent slowness of cleaning-up operations in different sectors and the deliberate movement of his four-pronged offensive aimed at Valencia, Castellon, Tarragona, and Barcelona. Whatever view may be taken of the military value of this caution, it must be regarded as evidence of the commander-in-chief's humanity toward his men. It is the key to the devotion of the Moors, who admired their leader's superb physical courage as much as his refusal to send them into battle until the staff-work had been completed.

Chivalry too plays its part in Franco's military outlook. While the Communist battalions were massing at Albacete prior to their brave defense of the Madrid outskirts, their movements and preparations were known to Franco. He realized that a few hours' delay at Toledo to relieve the defenders of the Alcazar might easily allow the foreigners to rally the half-hearted Republicans of the capital. Nevertheless, touched with admiration for the men, women and children in the historic fortress, General Franco turned aside to terminate the siege, a manoeuvre in which he was successful, but which gave the Communists just enough leeway to throw their forces in front of Madrid for the heroic stand which has captivated the imagination of millions throughout the world. Generalissimo Franco was the first to recognize a valiant foe.

To a soldier in love even war has to halt in order to give scope to romance. On October 16, 1923, Lieutenant-Colonel Francisco Franco, returning to the Iberian Peninsula, claimed as his bride his childhood sweetheart, Carmen Polo y Martinez Valdes, whom he had courted from the time he was twenty and she was fifteen. They met when Carmen was a school-girl, closely chaperoned, as is the custom in Spain, and daughter of a family deeply tinctured with pacifism.

"In my home," she related in after years, "we were all pacifists. Shortly after our *fiançialles* and wedding, my father was reading with passionate attention all the maps pertaining to the African war in which Francisco was participating."

The month-old honeymoon was terminated by a sudden return to the command of troops in Africa. Since that day, Carmen Polo de Franco has been the wife of a soldier and her daughter, Carmencita, the adored of the household, the child of a commander in the field.

Victory tripped on the heel of victory in Spanish Morocco until at the age of thirty-two, Francisco Franco, loaded with decorations from both Spain and France, was brevetted as the youngest General in Europe. It is significant that 90 per cent of the officers who had served with him in Africa had been killed in action. He could say not without an ordinate pride:

"I have seen death at my side many a time, but thanks to Heaven, it has not claimed me . . . "

He maintained his reputation as a leader who hated to risk the lives of his fellow Legionnaires, saving, as his biographer reports, (p. 93) "an infinite number of casualties." The soldiers, fully aware of this, were admiring, grateful.

"Climb the slopes with precaution, and on all fours to the last step when necessary, always ready to meet the enemy and to avoid being taken by surprise."

"The division shall never form in rigid order" and "The enemy never gets to his steel weapon except when the soldiers run" were other minutely-pencilled instructions to his men. Concentrated and serene, General Franco maintained confidence in himself and in his followers. Perhaps he remembered the maxim of Napoleon: "In the darkest hour of defeat and despair bear in mind that your enemy is more terrified than are you!"

The scene of Franco's success now moves to the General Military Academy at Saragossa. This bore the relation to the Academy at Toledo that our American War College bears to the Military School at West Point. In other words, the Saragossa center was a training-school of officers, destined for the more responsible positions in the army and on the General Staff. Franco is rightfully called the founder of this Academy.

One of his first acts was to draw up a Decalogue for the members of the college: Two precepts are conspicuous for their reflection of the spirit of the Director. They are:

(5) "Never to complain, nor to tolerate it . . .
(10) To be brave and self-sacrificing."

There was to be ample scope for the practice of both these virtues under the spasmodic government of the Republic, which was inaugurated by the flight of the King on April 14, 1931. Stool-pigeons and spies were in their heyday. The head of the Military Academy fell under official suspicion.

Before Franco took his departure into virtual exile, however, he bade farewell to his students in a speech of moving sincerity and beauty.

"In these times," he concluded, "when gentlemanliness and honor suffer constant rebuke, we have succeeded in making good our pride in being gentlemen, maintaining among you a *high spirituality.*"

Thereupon Manuel Azaña, at that time Minister of War and, prior to his tragic demise, the "forgotten man" as President of the so-called Spanish Republic, carried out his pseudo-humorous threat: "I will send him to the Balearic Islands so as to keep him out of temptation."

When the Anarchist revolt, however, endangered the Government, it was the signal for Franco's return to the Peninsula. Brigadier-General Franco was installed in the War Ministry. The battle against anarchy was under way. Franco was promoted to the responsible position of Chief of Staff. His talents were esteemed by the representative of the Popular Action Party, José Maria Gil Robles, Minister of War.

The elections of February 16, 1936, which restored the Left to power in the Cortez, were in actuality a majority victory for the Rightist elements at the polls. The popular will was nullified by intimidation, violence and fraud. As a consequence, the next six months constituted a veritable reign of terror.

Once more, Franco was dispatched into exile, this time with the connivance of the then-President of the Republic, now an unemployed, disillusioned journalist in Paris, Niceto Alcala Zamora. The President of the Republic bade him farewell. He dismissed the disorders and dismay of the country in these words:

"Don't worry, General. Don't worry. In Spain there will be no Communism."

"One thing that I am sure of," countered Franco, "and which I can affirm truthfully, is that whatever the contingencies that may arise here, wherever I am there will be no Communism."

From his isolated post in the Canary Islands, Gen. Franco made another pertinent observation. He said:

"When the funds of the workers' organizations are devoted to political bribery, the purchase of arms and munitions, and the hiring of gunmen and assassins, democracy, as represented by universal suffrage, has ceased to exist."

The rest of the story is contemporaneous history, or rather history in the making. How the swift airplane, the O-H-Rapide, arriving anonymously at Las Palmas from Croydon, waited for the hour of decision; how Franco at two ten P.M. on July 18, 1936, took off for Agadir, Casablanca and Tetuan; how he raised the standard of counter-revolution among the battalions of the Army of Africa; how he transported his troops by plane and boat across the Straits; how his valorous subordinates, Varela, Yagué and Mola brought about the union of the men of the North and the South in the plains about Avila; how the Alcazar was relieved and the provinces of Malaga, the Basque country, Aragon, Teruel, Catalonia and Valencia, were restored to Christian Spain,—all that is an epic that will no doubt inspire poet, orator and historian for centuries to come. It is a story of grandeur and glory, worthy of Ferdinand and Isabella, invoking the genius of a Cervantes, a Lope de Vega, a Velasquez and an Altamirano. It is a task, a labor of love to be entrusted to the heart and mind of a Spaniard.

Master of the forty-eight provinces of his native land, ruling benevolently and justly over three-quarters of her loyal sons and daughters, dealing wisely with foreign powers as well as with domestic difficulties, inseparable from the conduct of war, Generalissimo Francisco Franco fully merits the title, which his friends in the United States and Europe, with a firm realization of their historical responsibility, bestow upon him in his hour of triumphant progress toward national unity: the George Washington of rebel fame and the Marshal Foch of Christian Spain.

Viva España: Una, Grande, Libre!

CHAPTER XVII

FRANCISCO FRANCO

Charting Spain's Future

IN AN exclusive interview, Generalissimo Francisco Franco declared that the battle of peace would be ten times more difficult than the campaigns of wartime.

Manifesting an air of sober optimism, the head of the Spanish Government outlined the chief problems that confront his people, enumerating "education, health, labor legislation, agrarian reform and housing" as "the most pressing needs of the hour."

The interview took place in the Generalissimo's private resident in Burgos. His work room was filled with the reports of experts on social and economic problems. The desk was piled high with legal documents and correspondence. The Caudillo had just signed a number of reprieves and commutations for criminals condemned to capital punishment. In Spain Franco is known to be far more clement and generous, even to notorious gangsters, than is deemed prudent by the principal law officers of the State.

As the Generalissimo stepped forward to meet me, his features lit up with the smile which has captivated the hearts of his fellow citizens. His figure seemed sturdier and stronger than it had been on the occasion of our last meeting. His bearing reflected confidence without pride or presumption, while the piercing eyes of a born commander of men in the field looked out beneath a forehead aristocratic and scholarly.

In point of fact, Franco is the most democratic of men —one who, prior to his reluctant acceptance of supreme power, had exclusively occupied himself with matters of military technique and strategy. In the sphere of his own profession he was a savant, or intellectual, capable of directing the studies of those Spanish officers who were selected to undertake advanced work at the Saragossa War College. Now that Franco has been catapulted into the duties of statecraft, he has shown the same mastery of detail and power of intense application which made him the first soldier of Europe.

These were the impressions and recollections that crowded in upon my mind as I heard the Generalissimo insist that "only continued sacrifice could rebuild Spain's cities and recover her cultural patrimony." Speaking in rapid, rhythmic phrases, the Spanish chief of State continued:

"During the war, when you approached the University City suburb of Madrid, barbed wire, trenches and machine-guns blocked further progress. Now, once again, you are able to motor from Burgos to Madrid in a few hours and to enter the former war zone from the Capital proper.

"You know there are still some bombs and shells which have to be removed from the sites of former battles on the outskirts of the city. There are still roads and bridges to be restored.

"The Leftists handed over to us a legacy of destruction and ruin. Many buildings are being renewed to the very foundations. Much of the material for this purpose must be fabricated anew or imported from abroad. Our own factories, public utilities and plants need a thorough overhauling.

"In a country where granaries, storehouses and reserves were depleted during a period of war-time strain, it is imperative either to improvise material or to see the most necessary work retarded.

"Our problem at times has been, one might almost say, to invent or create equipment. Army engineers did something of the kind during the time of conflict; they cannot be expected to deal in magic or legerdemain now that peace has been won!"

This observation was made with a sense of quiet humor. Franco's eyes twinkled as he lapsed for a moment from the habitual gravity of the Spaniard. Then he added:

"Fortunately, we have restored hundreds of thousands of solid soldiers to private life. That is an achievement.

"Moreover, our Department of Public Works has a special section which aims to provide employment for the young men who have known the activity of swift campaigns and long hours of toil—who cannot be allowed to remain idle.

"As the head of the Spanish State, I am determined that every citizen who risked his life for the salvation of our people will be given a full opportunity to earn a good living."

The Generalissimo explained that thousands of men had been incorporated into road-building crews. He regards communications and transport in a mountainous country to be indispensable to the nation's orderly development. Due to the rugged, snow-capped Sierras, one village is as far from another in Spain, as one famous Spanish writer expressed it, "as Valladolid is from Ghent."

In vivid phrases, the Caudillo indicated his interest in public health and child welfare.

"Every army officer," he said, "knows the paramount importance of sanitation in camp or travel. Our hospital, medical and surgical facilities were expanded each and every day that we were engaged in warfare.

"What a tragedy it would be if this progress were to be interrupted! It is my intention personally to visit every province of Spain, there to undertake an investigation of health conditions.

"The first to benefit by this program will be the children—the future citizens of new Spain. The Conquistadores who explored the Americas were strong in soul and body. They had physical frames that could resist the diseases of tropical swamps and the almost incredible hardships of diet and travel. Spain's climate is not one that can tolerate weaklings.

"The magnificent work of the hundreds of thousands of volunteers in the *Auxilio Social* is a long step in the right direction. These generous auxiliaries have devoted their prime attention to young boys and girls. It is my conviction that the sound evolution of the *Auxilio Social* will improve the health of Spain's youngsters 50 percent within the next ten years. Milk, fruit, dairy products and bread bulk large in the dietary needs of the children.

"The leaders of the *Auxilio Social,* having conferred

with me, submitted a further program of exercise and recreation. This program has my cordial approval and support. I will spare no pains or expense to extend the influence of this thoroughly Christian organization, to which we were deeply indebted for war-time service."

Questioned about the length of time necessary to put his program into effect, Generalissimo Francisco Franco made a characteristic reply.

"Not long ago," he said, "people were curious about the duration of the siege of Madrid. They insisted that they must have precise information about the day and the hour that the Leftists would collapse. As a military man, accustomed to undertake tasks in the army spirit, I am less concerned about the time required to effect an operation than I am about the quality and permanence of the result."

"Spain," General Franco added, "is in no mood for mediocre performances or half-jobs. She is thinking in terms of empire, victory, splendid advances. The first conquest, therefore, must be in the domain of self. She must toil bravely to reconstruct what has been destroyed and at the same time usher in an era of social justice that will realize the teachings of Christ and the Vicars of Christ. Our best empire will be enriched living for the workers and the farmers of Spain."

CHAPTER XVIII

FRANCISCO FRANCO

His Social Program

Q. What attention has Your Excellency given to the principles of justice for the workingman enunciated by Leo XIII in the *Rerum Novarum* and by Pius XI in the *Quadragesimo Anno?*

A. As head of the Spanish nation, which looks to the Holy See for authoritative guidance in the supreme question of ethical and moral practice, I have naturally studied with profound attention the pronouncements of our religious leaders upon the proposed solutions to the evil of social injustice in the world. Obviously, the doctrines of the papal encyclicals furnish a sound program of social and economic reconstruction. The application of these principles, however, must be considered in relation to the genius and traditions of the Spanish people. For that reason a number of my collaborators are making a detailed study of the methods of application that would be suitable for Spain.

Of this you may be certain: we shall provide a living wage for every agricultural worker. Furthermore, the State will devise means to reward proportionately those who are charged with family responsibilities. I believe firmly in the principle of the family wage. One of our principal concerns in the midst of war has been the thorough preservation of family life. To the best of our ability we have avoided the necessity of conscripting the head of the house. In this respect our record contrasts favorably with that of our enemies who conscripted soldiers without regard to their social obligations.

The fact that the Holy See has been prompt to recognize the Nationalist Government and to receive the credentials of our diplomatic representative in Rome is a proof that the Vatican has entire confidence in our conscientious desire to carry out the recommendations of the *Rerum Novarum* and the *Quadragesimo Anno*. The factory workers in the great industrial center of Bilbao can give you first-hand testimony as to the efficacy of our program of economic reconstruction.

Q. Is Your Excellency prepared to state that Spain will recognize the right of the workers to a share in the profits of industry?

A. Both employers and employes will receive a share of the fruits of industrial production. This rule will apply to both native-born and foreign capitalists. If the latter refuse to conform to our ideal of justice, they will not be welcome in Spain.

Q. Does Your Excellency accept the principle that workers should be afforded a reasonable measure of security against the hazards of sickness, unemployment and old age?

A. Every enlightened nation gives its hearty support to this principle. Spain will be in the forefront of this movement. Anyone who has followed our history for the past twelve months knows that our first care has been for those members of the civil population who were wrenched from their homes and employment due to the conditions of anarchy and chaos which surrounded the victims of Red rule. Ask this question of the women and children who were rescued from starvation and suffering at Bilbao and Santander. They have experienced at first-hand the comforts of our policy of social security. On every hand the Spanish Army is hailed as the guarantee of peace and order, the indispensable pillars of social security.

Q. Is Your Excellency committed to the ideal of the corporative State?

A. This is a general term and may be easily misunderstood. Corporatism in Spain will grant to every citizen the right to participate in the social and economic life of the country on the basis of his labors. In other words, the prime requisite of civic responsibility will be function. In this way it will be possible to avoid the dangers which arise from corrupt politics or outmoded geographical divisions. I believe that this will be an effective antidote for separatism and particularism, two evils which have long plagued Spanish political life. Our Corporatism, however, will be indigenous, domestic, Spanish. It will be suited to the individualism of the Spanish personality. It will not be slavishly modeled upon foreign patterns. It should be noted, for example, that the system of corporations set up by Dr. Oliviera Salazar in Portugal is Iberian, not continental. We in Spain will fashion our own type of corporation in the arts, industry, agriculture and professions.

Q. Does Your Excellency believe that there would be any danger of excessive State regimentation in this corporative system?

A. The present administration of Spain shows that this danger may be kept far in the background. We have not interfered with any of the legitimate demands of private enterprise. Our sole purpose has been to prevent profiteering, the cancerous growth which springs from war and enriches a few at the expense of the great bulk of the population.

Every sincere foreign observer has commented upon the absence of profiteering in Nationalist Spain. Prices are altogether normal and in no case excessive. Indeed, there are some commodities which can be purchased at a price lower than that which was current at the outbreak of the war of liberation. This is not regimentation. It is a proper protection of the consuming public. To be sure profits of brokers, speculators and middlemen have been curtailed, but business has not suffered. Supplies of foodstuffs are plentiful and there is no hoarding, a phenomenon which usually accompanies armed conflict. The State has been vigilant in punishing any attempted case of gouging and as a result temptations to this form of exploitation are few.

The same principle applies to rents. Property-holders are entitled to a fair return of their investment, but they have not been permitted to engage in a wholesale kiting of rents. Revenues from property may be moderate but they have the advantage of steadiness and security. Naturally, we cannot speak of a large-scale housing program until all Spain has been liberated.

Q. What do you consider to be the principal needs of the farm population of Spain?

A. This question deserves thorough study. Lack of sufficient rainfall on the plateau regions of the peninsula makes the question of irrigation of pivotal importance. But irrigation postulates a huge volume of water in year-round rivers. This condition does not exist throughout Spain. What water is available must be carefully husbanded and utilized. Reforestation will be an undoubted boon. Diversification of crops, as in so many other countries, will also vastly improve the diet of the agricultural workers. Spain has the soil to produce rich crops of fruits and vegetables. A larger proportion of this produce should be consumed on the farm. Dairy production can likewise be stepped up to an enormous extent. We have grazing land in plenty and an excellent grade of stock animals. There is no reason why the exercise of creative imagination should not work miracles for the large number of Spaniards who till the soil. Modern machinery and scientific farm knowledge will complete the transformation.

Q. What will be the trade policy of Spain under Your Excellency's régime?

A. Spain will show a vigorous leadership in the restoration of world trade. Up to the present, in spite of the severe strain of daily war, Spain has financed herself from the sale of products abroad. As a result there has been a just balance between imports and exports. Spanish iron, wool, cork and olive oil are highly prized articles of export. On the other hand, Spain is an admirable market for textiles, electrical apparatus, farm machinery and automobiles. Buying and selling is of the essence of trade. Spain is prepared to continue both on a sound basis of cash and credit.

We have no desire to be isolated from world economy. And we believe the reciprocal trade treaties of the United States of America, especially as they have been operative with South American countries, furnish interesting examples of how national benefits may be articulated with the trade exigencies of good neighbors. Spain too has excellent cultural and economic relations with the Republics of South America.

Q. What guarantees of religion does Your Excellency provide in Spain?

A. Spain guarantees complete religious liberty, as opposed to mere religious toleration, to all who believe in God. There will be no penalties in the realm of conscience. In fact, a high realization of religious and moral values is the most helpful motivation for a program of social justice. Advances in material civilization will be taken step by step with progress in the cultivation of spiritual ideals. These two bear the relationship of soul and body. The hearts and minds of Spaniards will guide their hands in the task that lies before them.

CHAPTER XIX

FRANCISCO FRANCO

Will He Be King?

THERE ARE three distinct currents of opinion with respect to a restoration of the Spanish royal house.

The first, warmly advocated by the dukes and marquises of the realm, is that monarchy is a sovereign remedy for all ills; the second, more realistic, considers that, although a king upon his throne is an admirable symbol of national unity, no one should be invited to assume royal prerogatives and royal responsibility until the major problems of the nations shall have been solved; while the third view, widely held among the rank and file of the Falange, is that kings, queens and princelings are a vain extravagance for an impoverished, struggling people.

In other words, a blind adherence to royalty is the badge of aristocrats and grandees; the majority of officers and soldiers in the army believe that, though a return to the monarchy is inevitable, it is at present inexpedient as well as premature; and a great body of inarticulate opinion demands concentration upon better food, clothing and housing prior to any further discussion of political formulas.

149

It can be stated categorically that the throne was never offered to the late King Alfonso XIII. From sources close to Generalissimo Francisco Franco, this correspondent learned that the question was never debated in Cabinet Council.

To be sure, none of the ministers are unsympathetic to the monarchical ideal: they would all vote in favor of royal restoration the moment they could feel sure that the time was ripe. But they, better than any Spaniards in the peninsula, are aware of the gravity and magnitude of Spain's real problems. Titular leadership is not one of them. A king and a court are simply not matters of immediate concern or urgency.

And the more far-sighted friends of the royal house are convinced that, if a sovereign were installed with traditional pageantry, he would straightway become the cynosure of all eyes at home and abroad and the potential scapegoat for criticism, no matter how slight or temporary the régime's setbacks might prove to be.

Speaking on this subject, an official known to enjoy the confidence of Sr. Serrano Suñer, brother-in-law of Franco, dropped a broad hint as to extreme reserve displayed by the Cabinet apropos of royalist agitation. He declared:

"This would be the worst possible moment to negotiate for a return of a monarch, not only because of the recent European war, but also because there has been a severe, if natural reaction to the wave of enthusiastic effort which ended the war. Franco's campaign in Catalonia was a climax finish to a long drawn-out, painful struggle. Every man and woman was girded for the final blow. Once that had been struck and victory had been secured, the very people who had been most alert, active and generous sank back into a sort of delicious torpor; they were prepared to drink deeply of the cup of triumph.

"A good many of the best fighters and workers had kept going on their nerves, and they have enjoyed their post-war repose. This constitutes a genuine danger for the task of reconstruction. Schools, homes and power-houses are not built by oratory in the casinos, cafes and clubs. The temptation to "erect castles in Spain" in the domain of the imagination would return in a highly exaggerated degree the moment a Bourbon would stride through the gates of the royal palace in Madrid.

"Twenty-two million Spaniards would sit back in the gallery to watch the king and his counsellors grapple with disease, penury, dirt. During the war every Spaniard realized that his role was that of protagonist, not a mere spectator. The most important function of government is to maintain the conviction of the common man that he is drama and theater, playwright, producer and cast. After all, a king is a poor substitute for wide-awake citizens!"

This frank expression of opinion confirmed the observations of this correspondent in some regions of Spain. The let-down after the great-hearted exertions of the war was particularly notable in Toledo. This one-time capital of Spain, affectionately called "the Imperial City," is just beginning to recuperate after having been digging itself out of the dust and debris which cluttered up almost every street during the siege of the Alcazar.

The principal square, atop the proud hill which overlooks the Tagus River, is still a picture of desolation. No one has had the energy to cover the drab nakedness of the park benches with a coat of paint. The smells and odors in narrow, tortuous streets do more than remind the traveler of centuries of Moorish occupation; they suggest powerfully that the drains are clogged with decaying cats, mice and unused vegetables.

More than a decade ago, that gifted Spanish intellectual, Don José Ortega y Gasset, pointed out that "Imperial Toledo" for all its traditions of grandeur could boast no monuments worthy of preservation save the Cathedral and the Alcazar. Apart from the loss of a number of window treasures, the Cathedral rises from the crowded space in the center of the city more glorious than ever; the Alcazar, though razed to its foundations, will remain one of the most fascinating of Spain's national museums. Otherwise, Ortega y Gasset's poignant criticism is still in order.

A street on the fringe of the city was being widened and straightened. That may be a sign of new vitality and determination. If so, the *Toledanos* can emulate with profit the example of the citizens and municipal government of Madrid. Until the reconstructive spirit of the capital shall have pervaded every level of Spanish life, the triumphant entry of His Most Catholic Majesty into the place of his forefathers would be at best an empty gesture. Under the present circumstances it is the conviction of the majority of Spaniards that crown and scepter are a senseless luxury.

CHAPTER XX

COLONEL FULGENCIO BATISTA

President of Cuba

IN AN exclusive interview accorded this writer, Colonel Fulgencio Batista, president of Cuba, declared that "in the present crisis of world affairs, especially as they touch upon the life and welfare of the American Republics, there must be a growing recognition of the supreme importance of spiritual forces and movements."

He insisted that "the imperishable value of the human soul" was "essentially linked with the destiny of democratic government in the Western Hemisphere," and that "those citizens who believe in these ideals could render a service to God and country by strengthening of the ties of friendship among spiritually-minded peoples in the United States and Cuba."

He called spiritual principles "the first line of national defense." The Cuban President added that in his opinion there was a "close connection between religious liberty and political freedom," a declaration similar to that made early last year in President Franklin D. Roosevelt's initial message to the Congress of the United States.

This correspondent was presented by United States Ambassador George S. Messersmith, who accompanied

153

him to the Presidential Palace in the heart of Havana. President Batista, who speaks English with correctness and fluency, greeted the Americans who came to him in their own language. The interview, itself, however, took place in Spanish. Ambassador Messersmith, who is proficient in that tongue, remained for the entire conference, which lasted almost an hour.

The interview took place in President Batista's private office, which is simple and unpretentious. His visitors were seated at a conference table which is used from time to time for more intimate meetings of Cabinet officers. President Batista's replies to inquiries displayed marked intuitive grasp of domestic and international problems. He did not do any hedging or try to evade issues by the familiar device of off-the-record statements.

In discussing his position with respect to religion, for example, President Batista was explicit in his citation of the nation's recently formulated Constitution which stipulates separation of Church and State and equality before the law for the members of all religious organizations.

"Cuban Catholics, both clergy and laity, took an active and vital interest in the drafting of the new Constitution. As adopted, the new Constitution contains nothing that positively favors the Church, but it does not encroach upon her rights and affords her the same protection of the Law as any other public society.

(Its invocation proclaims the existence of God, and the body of the Constitution assures freedom of worship, protects private religious education and, on the whole, recognizes Christian morality as the norm of public morality.)

"Although the Constitution of Cuba is emphatic in providing a lay State, it does not and cannot deny the essentially Christian genius of our people," President Batista explained, adding that in his "innermost soul," he was persuaded of the powerful influence which moral principles could have in promoting economic reconstruction and social justice.

"The desire for security among the workers," President Batista declared, "springs from a realization that the human personality has a noble origin and lofty purpose. Citizens conscious of the soul's higher aspirations will labor for a more equitable distribution of wealth and income without infringing upon the rights of their fellow men. The divine element which they wish respected in themselves will impel them to recognize its counterpart in others. Equity in the civic sense has a spiritual foundation.

"Now, more than ever, when troubles multiply, even for the innocent, in a war-torn world, it is imperative to reassert the claims of the spirit. Materialism is inadequate; animalism leads to brutality; the antidote to both is to be sought in the dynamics of the soul. For the citizen, aware of his soul, is awake to the demands of his conscience. It is only in the domain of conscience that right conquers wrong, that spiritual realities overcome mere physical force."

The Cuban executive expressed keen interest and sympathy in the program of cultural studies on Latin-America which his visitors outlined.

CHAPTER XXI

MOST REVEREND GEORGE J. CARUANA

Papal Nuncio to Cuba

"THE CATHOLIC CHURCH in Cuba is on the threshold of great developments," declared His Excellency the Most Reverend George J. Caruana, Papal Nuncio to Cuba, in an interview given to this correspondent.

"The people of Cuba," he stated, "are intensely receptive to the ministrations of the Catholic Faith, and the Government has shown itself favorably disposed to admit full freedom of religious worship and activity."

During the interval since the death of the Archbishop of Havana, the Papal Nuncio has personally attended to the work of confirming in the various villages as well as in capital city and is thoroughly conversant with the problems of the Cuban people. The decline of the sugar market and the practical closing down of the export cigar industry, particularly since the war started have, as he indicated, caused wide-spread unemployment throughout the island and intensified the problem of subsistence among the poorer classes. Nevertheless, the native geniality of the people has kept up their traditional optimism and, if anything, has increased their desire for religion.

At the same time, Catholic Action has organized itself to a remarkable degree, notably among the youth. The Nuncio expressed special gratification with the professional and scholastic groups that have been formed by Catholic lay leaders in connection with the University and various centers of learning. Work also is being done among the laboring classes, by young men and women, along the Jocist lines previously developed in Belgium and France; and catechetical instructions are given by qualified students, particularly where there are not sufficient priests. Thus in Havana itself classes are held in one parish in which there is only one priest for 120,000 souls.

The principal obstacle in the way of progress, according to Archbishop Caruana, is the dearth of priests and in particular of native vocations. There are fewer than 600 clergy for the total population of 4,500,000. When it is recalled that a large percentage of these are engaged in teaching or are attached as chaplains to the various institutions serving charitable purposes, the problem of meeting the pastoral needs of the Island becomes extremely grave.

One of the most serious considerations in this respect is the cost of educating young men for the priesthood, since this preparation must begin in the more elementary grades, with a corresponding loss of applicants before the final courses of philosophy and theology can be given.

The Nuncio declared that much good has been accomplished by scholarships established for Cuban students, both boys and girls, by Catholic institutions in the United States and expressed the belief that this form of cooperation could be of great service in promoting a wholesome solidarity among the nations of the Western Hemisphere. The traditional culture of the Latin-American peoples, he pointed out, is profoundly Catholic, and this fact must be taken into consideration if friendly relations are to be maintained on a positive basis in the future.

An American citizen for many years, but a native of the island of Malta, Archbishop Caruana recalled with pride that he served as chaplain in the forces of the United States during the World War. As an envoy of the Vatican, he later represented the Church in Mexico and Guatemala before his appointment in Cuba, and he is therefore well acquainted with the problems and aspirations of the Latin-American countries.

While commenting with optimism on the cordial spirit of the Cuban government, to which he is accredited as dean of the diplomatic corps, he mentioned also the helpful attitudes of the American ambassadors, including the present representative, Ambassador George S. Messersmith, and his predecessor, Ambassador J. H. Jefferson Caffery, to whom he referred as a man whose devout Catholic faith as well as representative statesmanship brought a new understanding of the Cuban people and served as an inspiration and stabilizing influence during transitional years of the Republic.

(Note. This interview was accorded jointly to the writer and his two colleagues on this occasion, the Reverend Dr. John A. Weidinger, associate professor of philosophy at Mount St. Mary's College, Emmitsburg, Maryland, and the Reverend Dr. James A. Magner, a member of the Institute of Ibero-American Studies at the Catholic University of America, Washington, D.C.)

CHAPTER XXII

HUEY P. LONG

A Tribune of the People?

As THIS writer was entering the over-size suite of offices occupied by Huey P. Long in the Senate Office Building, Will Rogers was making a triumphal exit. The office force of the Senator from Louisiana was enjoying a major thrill, because the Oklahoma cowboy and erstwhile Mayor of Beverly Hills, California, was dispensing his autograph to blondes and brunettes with princely generosity. As he reached the door and turned around for a final greeting, his eyes twinkled for a moment and then with a characteristic wave of his hand he shouted: "So long, girls; I'll see you in the White House!"

One thing is certain: The Hollywood cowboy fitted into the picture in the Long headquarters. On the surface there was the same circus atmosphere to which radio listeners and Senate galleries had long since grown accustomed. Informality and friendliness were in the air. Everybody, of course, was working, but no one seemed to be under a strain. Batteries of typewriters pounded out answers to the thirty-thousand odd letters that poured in each day. Shipping clerks prepared piles of books and pamphlets for mailing. (*Every Man a King*

159

was still in demand.) A Railway Express freight clerk wandered in and out with his truck. Waste baskets were filled to overflowing, while empty envelopes and blue and yellow telegram containers littered the floor.

Telephone bells rang almost incessantly. The nearest stenographer or secretary picked up the receiver. "Senator Long's office," soon dinned itself into the memory like the refrain of a popular song. The scene abounded in paradoxes. Outside, for example, tacked to the door, was a pencil-printed sign: "We Regret Very Much That We Cannot Receive Visitors Today." Nevertheless, there was a constant tattoo of knocks at the door. Some visitors were admitted; others were advised to come on the morrow. A few were obviously on the inner circle; these were asked: "Do you want to see Earl or the *Boss?*" Earl was Mr. Earl Christenberry, Senator Long's secretary. Nattily attired Western Union and Postal Telegraph messenger boys shuttled in and out. Indeed, they were the most frequent visitors, receiving and delivering high-speed messages. When telegrams were dispatched, usually by Mr. Christenberry, they went out in sheaves.

So much had been written about the fact that every letter to Senator Long received a personal reply that it was interesting to add this correspondent's observations. A friendly secretary invited him into one of the side rooms. It was a beehive of activity. At least fifteen girls, ranging in age from eighteen to twenty-five, were seated around a large table. Spread out before them were the contents of the last mail sack. The girls were reading and sorting the letters. Those which pertained to the

"Share-the-Wealth" clubs went into one box; those seeking pamphlets or speeches went into another.

In this way, it would be correct to say that the huge volume of mail was, in the language of the blood-test experts, "typed." No doubt there were excellent standardized replies. The girls worked in two shifts: about twenty-two carried on during the day and perhaps eighteen at night. Not infrequently, the office secretary came in to announce: "There is such a crush of work that it will be necessary to work overtime this evening." The only responses to this announcement were sighs and wan smiles of resignation. The Louisianian's office was not a stenographers' paradise.

At this point, Congressman Sam Steagall (he was rumored as Secretary of the Treasury in the Senator's future hypothetical Cabinet) emerged and your correspondent was ushered into the private office. The interview was under way without formality or delay.

"Senator," your correspondent remarked, "the people of America are particularly interested in your views of Father Charles E. Coughlin. What are your relations with the Detroit priest?"

"Father Coughlin," replied Senator Long, "is a good friend of mine. I like him. I won't say we work together, because that would denote an alliance or combination. But I will say that he is fighting for the same general objectives that I am. He believes that in this world of depression and business stagnation the emphasis should be placed on social justice. So do I. I believe in social justice and I will continue to fight for my program."

Believing that the public would wish to know wherein the Senator's program differed, if at all, from that of Father Coughlin, this writer put that question.

"Well, there isn't so much difference," declared Senator Long. "I don't disagree with Father Coughlin very often; in fact, we disagree very seldom. Nor are our differences fundamental or important. I would almost say that we are working for practically the same principles each in our own way. Father Coughlin has his method and style; I have mine. But when you come right down to it, I don't think there is a great deal of difference.

"In that case, Senator," your correspondent urged, "you will not oppose the bill for centralized banking introduced in the Senate by Senator Gerald P. Nye. You know the latter expressly stated that Father Coughlin had been one of those consulted about the bill. Are you planning to support this legislation?"

At first, the Senator from Louisiana did not wish to commit himself too absolutely upon this proposition, but finally he admitted that, since he was in general agreement with Father Coughlin on most things, he might be presumed to be in favor of the Nye banking bill. To say the least, it was clear that there was between the two leaders a fairly satisfactory understanding, if not a working agreement.

All this, of course, was preliminary to a much more important and somewhat more controversial question.

"Senator Long," your correspondent queried, "how do you account for the fact that Father Coughlin in his broadcast refutation of General Hugh Johnson appeared to climb back on the Administration band wagon?

Why, in spite of his severe criticism of President Roosevelt's New Deal, did the Detroit radiorator reverse his field and apparently dash back on the reservation?"

At this pointed question, sparks began to fly in the *Sanctum Sanctorum*. The chief open adversary of the Roosevelt Administration struggled to restrain his vehemence. He succeeded. There was intense subdued feeling in his reply.

"I'm not so sure," he drawled slowly and a bit ironically, "that Father Coughlin ran back to the reservation. Didn't he declare that he would continue to criticize what was wrong in the President's program and accept only what he thought was sound and beneficial? Personally, I don't see any difference in his attitude before or after that speech. He's just the same, I think. I think he'll go right along as he was before and so will I."

After a brief interlude in which the Senator described his first introduction to Father Coughlin, the stage was set for another question.

"Mr. Long," it was suggested, "do you often see the good Father from Detroit? Does he confer with you or you with him when he comes to the capital?"

There was no doubt or hesitation or equivocation about the answer to this query.

"Certainly, I see him most every time he comes to Washington. We are good friends. He almost always has a visit with me. He's like my other good friend, Will Rogers. Will wouldn't think of coming to the Capital without visiting me. I'm always glad to see Father Coughlin and I think he feels the same way about me."

With this much clear, it seemed proper and profitable to enlarge the bases of the discussion.

"Senator Long," your correspondent suggested, "everybody is interested in the more equitable distribution of wealth. Both you and Father Coughlin have that in common. But isn't that the same general objective for all interested in securing social justice? Several magazines and reviews, for example, recently featured an interview by a staff member with Hilaire Belloc. Belloc expressed the liberal economic views which he has championed for many years. He calls his system that of distribution. What do you think of his program? How does it compare with your own? What is your mature judgment of the distribution of wealth advocated by Belloc?"

"What is his name?"

"Hilaire Belloc, the British historian and philosopher," your correspondent repeated, endeavoring to cover his embarrassment at this unexpected blind spot revealed on the Senatorial retina.

"Never heard of him," the Senator proclaimed, "I don't know anything about his program. What does Belloc propose?"

This is not an interview with Belloc on his "Share-the-Wealth" system and so there is no need to insert the familiar explanation of the Chesterbelloc program. But this much must be said for Mr. Long. He listened attentively, his eyes flashing, to every detail of the Belloc proposal and did not hesitate to subjoin at the end:

"It sounds all right to me. I wish I knew more about it."

Eager to get the gentleman from Louisiana back to more familiar territory, your correspondent made a reference to a recent radio speech delivered by the Senator himself.

"It was interesting, Mr. Long, to hear you declare that your Share-the-Wealth plan had been advocated by every important leader in all times. You put at the head of this list the Holy Father in the Vatican. May I ask whether you, Senator, have read the two celebrated Encyclical Letters, namely, the *Rerum Novarum* of Leo XIII and the *Quadragesimo Anno* of Pius XI?"

"Have I read them!" roared the Senator. "I was the one who put them in the *Congressional Record*. I had them inserted in the *Record*. Certainly, I did that a long time ago. And I quote the Pope in my book. Here it is!"

At this point, Senator Long rang for Christenberry to bring in a copy of "Share Our Wealth," but finding one on the desk he was able to dismiss his secretary and point out the passage from *"Quadragesimo Anno"* which appeared on page 27. It was obvious that the Senator was as proud of this quotation as if it were a personal endorsement from the white-robed ruler of Vatican City.

Naturally, your correspondent wished to follow up such a fruitful subject of conversation.

"Senator Long, in view of your careful reading of the Encyclical *Quadragesimo Anno,* what would you be able to tell the citizens of America about your opinion of one of the most important of the Holy Father's *specific* recommendations, namely, that favoring the organization of *occupational groups* in the various industries, trades, arts and professions?"

"That is a part of the document which I have not read," the Senator replied. "I don't know anything about it. But it sounds like NRA. If it's NRA, I'm against it. But I really haven't studied that section of the Pope's letter and so I really don't know."

We also discussed this country's policy with regard to Mexico, Soviet Russia, Europe and the Administration's legislative program of domestic recovery but this interview is already too long. A great deal could also be written with respect to flaming, white-hot personal impressions of the leader of the Opposition, but perhaps, in view of events, may best be left under the head of "Unfinished Business."

CHAPTER XXIII

TRUE INTERNATIONALISM

Brotherhood in God

"THERE ARE no political settlements; there are religious solutions."

This statement was made to me, some eight years ago, by one of the American delegates to the Geneva World Conference "for the Limitation and Reduction of Armaments." The very title of the meeting suggests how futile was the debate of politicians in 1932. What was meant to be the starting-point toward smaller armies and navies became a springboard for higher quotas in every category of arms. A single statesman from one of the Great Powers mentioned the name of God. His invocation of Providence was swept away in the tide of selfish nationalism. The Geneva "Disarmament" Conference touched the low-water mark of secular politics.

True internationalism is built upon souls. All peoples and all nations are called to the construction of a world society. True security is soul-security. The American citizen, conscious of his responsibility before God for the salvation of souls in America, China and Japan, is steeped in the philosophy of peace and fired with a passion for world welfare. The image of God, stamped on each soul, inspires love, understanding and generosity.

An analogy may help to illustrate this point. Every nation in the world may be pictured in the imagination as surrounded by two walls, one of flesh and one of spirit. The weaker the wall of spirit, the higher must rise the wall of flesh. The stronger the wall of spirit, the more easily and more securely may it dispense with the outlying wall of steel.

Between many countries there have been erected military, naval and economic barriers which testify to the instability of the moral factors of security. Between others there are miles and miles of unguarded frontier. Here moral security is the wall of spirit. Fearless and far-sighted statesmanship, for example, negotiated the Rush-Bagot Agreement of 1818 dismantling the gunboats which had begun to be launched on the Great Lakes and providing that the continental boundary of the United States and Canada, which is now more than 3,000 miles in length, should henceforth be undefended by frontiers, fortresses, garrisons or guns. We have had many disputes since that time with our Canadian neighbors, and we have had many attempts on the part of militarists and ship-builders to annul the agreement; but the two nations, cherishing their common Christian heritage, have adhered loyally to their pact of friendship. In the absence of preparations to settle their disputes by war, they have succeeded in settling them all by the peaceful processes of arbitration and conciliation. This was to carry out in practice the recommendation of Benedict XV who never ceased to extoll the virtues of "the noble instrument of arbitration."

So too, in South America, Argentine and Chile, after a series of wars, threats of war and actual preparation for war, in 1902, by the disarmament of a thousand miles of their mutual frontier and the adoption of universal arbitration, showed that for every increase of moral protection it was possible to dispense with a proportionate amount of physical security. Instead of stocking the mountain heights with howitzers and machine gun posts, they made from their discarded cannon a colossal statue of the Prince of Peace and erected it upon a snow-capped border peak of the Andes, 13,000 feet above sea level, to remind the two nations of their agreement, and to declare that "sooner shall these mountains crumble into dust than the people of Argentine and Chile break the peace which they have sworn to maintain at the feet of Christ the Redeemer."

Obviously, the most important single factor in moral security is sincere acceptance of the teachings of the Divine Founder of Christianity. Where issues are studied under the flood lights of Christian justice and charity there can be no danger of an outbreak of armed hostilities. The individual citizen is not primarily a voter, or an office-holder, or a soldier; fundamentally, he is a creature of God, the Father: a brother of Christ, the Redeemer: the Beloved of the Holy Spirit, Sanctifier of souls.

Having fed upon "Grapes of Wrath," soldiers and statesmen forget that they have had spread before them the crowning banquet of life, "Grapes on the Vine." Souls, sprinkled with the Blood of Christ, are saved. They need no other shedding of blood. For the Redeemer is not only the Christ of the Andes, but also the Christ of the Alps, the Pyrenees, the Urals, the Rockies and the Himalayas: He is the Christ of the Rhine, the Ganges, the Yangtze and the Nile. His sword is Justice; His rallying-cry remains Charity. "Savior of the Universe" blazes on His banners. It is in supreme allegiance to Him that all other loyalties, devotions and sacrifices can enjoy validity.

His Holiness, Pius XII, has shown Himself the Vicar of the Christ of all Continents. Almost His first act was to renew the reality of the Apostolic College by consecrating Bishops—twelve representatives of diverse races and nations. No church under Heaven could afford a similar spectacle. In a world scourged by petty hates, the Vicar of the Redeemer displayed the symbol of the world apostolate. Undismayed by "wars and rumors of wars," His Holiness revivified the principle of Oneness in Divine Grace. Pius XII takes His place with Pius XI as "the Pope of the missions."

Security for the individual must precede security for the nation or for the world. Family stability is closely linked with personal holiness. For that reason, security in the full sense of the term must be builded on the firm basis of supernatural religion, knowing absolutely no frontiers and uniting peoples of the most diverse race, condition and temperament by the inward bonds of sacramental grace, indivisible truth and obedience to the same spiritual authority. Statesmen whose efforts were in a contrary direction, whose boast it was that they "had put out the lights of Heaven" did nothing but prepare their fellow citizens for two disastrous world wars. The secular State can never provide, and is not intended to provide, that indispensable, transcendent, spiritual element of security that flows from religious principles firmly imbedded in the hearts and minds of the people.

To be sure, peoples are ranged on opposite sides in wars raging both in the Orient and in the Occident. Christians fight in the ranks for their respective Governments. Unfortunately, Catholic Christians are in a minority on both sides in both wars. They are subordinated to the secular institutions and secular hatreds of the times. But they openly profess that their highest loyalty is to God; they acknowledge that the love of Christ is applicable to those styled "enemies" and that conversion to Christianity is the way to end slaughter. Right principles are a prelude to right conduct.

In other words, truth is antecedent to practice of the virtues, even to the operation of justice and charity. And what truth is more important than Revelation? Who are more precious than those who bring the tidings of great joy? What is the message that can introduce the golden thread of unity into history, law, art and the other elements of culture? The truth comes first! Fairness and affection are its corollaries, if the Truth is Divine. In this sense, the missionaries, whether priests or nuns or lay people, are the best builders of a sound international order. They are the advance-guard of the true internationalism. They are living the reality of the spiritual League of Nations. They are the exponents of a true Society of States.

Patriotic in their devotion to their native land, the missionaries are none the less loyal to the people of Christ's predilection. Whether they labor in Shanghai or Bombay, these internationalists *par excellence* give a practical example of mankind's solidarity. Neither Fascist, nor Nazi, nor Communist, they dispense their riches (often a mere pittance) to all without distinction of color or culture. Neither capitalistic nor proletarian, they create a home for coolies as well as mandarins. They are the soul of what social order remains in the world.

It is encouraging to note the growth of supernatural, supra-national internationalism in the Catholic high schools, colleges and universities of America. Catholic youth are convinced that God is the best guarantee of democratic liberties. Wherever a strong mission spirit grows, one is sure to find clubs and societies devoted to the study of world problems. (Units of the Catholic Students' Peace Federation dot the land.) American young men and young women are interesting themselves in the destiny of members of the *Pax Romana*, especially those now in the crucible of war. Spread of the Faith is universally recognized as the touchstone of a new international order.

When Duns Scotus, himself a renowned university scholar of his age, died in 1308, the following words were inscribed above his tomb:

"Scotia me genuit	*"Ireland bore me,*
Gallia me docuit	*France taught me*
Anglia me suscepit	*Britain heard me*
Colonia me tenet."	*Cologne keeps me."*

The Catholic youth of America understand this inscription. They are trying to translate its ethos into substantial support for the domestic and foreign missions. They are convinced that the world of tomorrow needs "One Lord, one Faith, one Baptism."

CHAPTER XXIV

MARY—OUR MOTHER

The Road of Security—to Jesus

To think of our mother makes us love all goodness. And in that love two excellencies are conspicuous: first, that our mother has been from tenderest years a symbol of purity, and, second, that she has likewise been the one human person in creation about the reality of whose devotion there has never been any doubt.

Friends will desert us; acquaintance shun us; and strangers repeat slanders about our name. But the mother who in pain brought us into the world, who shielded us against bodily and spiritual hurt in childhood and prepared us for life's larger struggles, does not know what it is to change or to waver. She is like that terrestial beauty lyricized by the poet, Wordsworth, "fair as a star when only one is shining in the sky."

If all this and more is true of our earthly mother, how much more abundantly is the description verified in the case of our Mother, who is in Heaven. Mary Immaculate, Star of the Sea, Consoler of the Afflicted, and Strength of the Weak is more than a tower of beauty in the bright morning of the world. To the tempted she is the first and most vigilant of the guardian angels; to the sinner she is a pledge of repentance; to the continent she is a daily inspiration; and to the valiant she is sword and shield.

In other words, the Virgin Mother, combining the most supernatural features of finite sanctity, is a Little Flower of Lisieux to soldiers in the ranks, an Elizabeth of Hungary to the unemployed and the poor, a St. Theresa of Avila to mystical souls, striving for further perfection, a St. Madeleine-Sophie Barat to modern maidens, and a Queen and Mother to all without exception.

What is the source of this sanctity and strength? Nothing more or less than constant, intimate, loving association with her Divine Son. Her privilege it was to learn the sweet mysteries of His Sacred Heart—in joy and in sorrow, in tranquil labor at Nazareth, in storm and persecution on Golgotha. In truth, Jesus and Mary were never separated—for distance is nothing when one is sure of love. And in that union of hearts there was, over and above everything else, purity and confidence— shall we say, unlimited confidence because of sinlessness?

What does Holy Scripture report of this fact? When the Archangel Gabriel, herald of the Blessed Trinity, announced to Mary that she was to be the Mother of God, what was the first instinct of her heart? Her vow of virginity! And the corollary? Perfect trust in the Divine Wisdom! "Behold the handmaid of the Lord. Be it done unto me according to Thy Word."

In the cave at Bethlehem was the scene less compelling? The Son in the arms of His Mother has won hearts that the King and Conqueror never could have touched. Why? Because it is an ideal of selflessness in love that is irresistible and that can never lose its appeal. It is an image of the "Greater love than this no man hath" of the Cross on Calvary, a foreshadowing of the sacrifice and suffering that are inseparable from the existence of a mother. Why has Bethlehem such fervent, timeless eloquence? Because there is no power on earth can destroy the trust an infant has for the breast of its mother.

Thus far, this is a portrayal of Mother and Son taken by themselves. What shall we say of Jesus and Mary as an inspiration to purity and confidence in their relations to the outside world?

The first act of the Saviour's public life, as we know, was His miracle at the marriage festival of Cana. It was His canonization of family life and the placing of a Divine seal upon the bond of Holy Matrimony. When word came from the head of the table that there was "no more wine," you may be sure that the hardship, self-denial, and sacrifice not incompatible with wedded bliss were vividly present to His mind. Yet He did not lift a finger. It was Mary who took the initiative in this generous determination to spare embarrassment to the youthful bride and groom as well as to warm the hearts of the wedding party.

Was the Mother's prayer not a prayer of confidence? "Son," she gently remarked, "they have no wine." It was no want of her own that she presented but that of others. It was hardly more than a simple statement of fact—"they have no wine." It is said that the mother of Herbert Cardinal Vaughn, saintly woman that she was, never requested from God any temporal favor for her children, not even fine weather for an outing or a journey. But the Mother of Christ did not hesitate to ask temporal favors and, having made petition, directed the master of the feast to do whatever Her Divine Son would ordain. How could she doubt but that her intercession would be efficacious? In spite of what appeared at first blush a dignified refusal, she was aware of the sentiments of the God-man and what would be the response of that Sacred Heart. Did she perhaps foresee that many human creatures in hours of need or weakness, in desire or hope, would also find a way to reach Jesus through the Immaculate Heart of His Mother?

At any rate, the water jars were filled to the brim, the master of the festival tasted the precious liquor, and the guests could not contain their admiration and praise: "They have kept the best wine for the last!" It was a simple reward, the Divine blessing on the married state, an inspiration to implicit trust in the Most Pure Heart of Mary.

Purity of heart often means, at least for a time, that we give up some prized object of possession. It may impose definite limitations on choice or remove from our presence a cherished companion. Our Lady knew this privation well. When Her Son went forth to His sacred ministry, she for the most part had to follow him only with prayer and affection. For the salvation and sanctification of mankind she postponed the enjoyment of His smile, His words of personal comfort, His practical help in the tiny house of Nazareth.

Like many others, she was not on hand, so far as we can learn from the Gospel narrative, to witness the baptism by John or the benediction of the Holy Spirit at the Jordan. Was she present for the miraculous multiplication of the loaves and the promise of the Eucharist? Were her ears gladdened by the joyful message of the Sermon on the Mount or consoled by the praise of the daughter of Jairus? We may be certain she did not glimpse the glory of the Transfiguration on Mt. Thabor. Nor have we any record that she was part of the exultant multitude who greeted Jesus as the Son of David and King of the Jews on the Festival of Palms. The Virgin, full of grace though she was, was not destined to share in earthly royal crowns or temporal triumphs. Was it to indicate that sinlessness and humility and sacrifice are closely akin one to the other?

Mary was no dazzling part of the theatrical, fleeting glory of the Messianic kingdom on earth, which the Jews vainly imagined. Perhaps her only glimpse of natural power and majesty in Her Son during this period was His teaching among the doctors of the law in the Temple. And that scene had been paid for in the anguish that preceded the finding of the Divine Child. But Mary was a witness of the bloody way that led from the Pretorium to the storm-swept heights of Calvary; her eyes beheld the institution of the Blessed Eucharist at the Last Supper; and she was privileged to participate in the immolation of the victim of infinite price upon the Cross.

Happily, the story does not end there. The climax of suffering and privation preceded an eternity of reward. To Mary was granted the favor of the first glimpse of the Risen Saviour. She enjoyed His radiant presence throughout forty days following the Resurrection. They were days of fulfillment and Easter peace.

And by the time she stood with the disciples on the Mount of the Ascension she had exchanged hope of better things for the certainty of unending joy.

No doubt there is a sort of rugged justice in the number and variety of the mysteries of the Most Holy Rosary of Our Lady. Of these, five speak of suffering and sacrifice. But by a happy preponderance, ten relate joys and announce glory. There is no overemphasis of tragedy or death in the Christian revelation. It is rather a magnificent drama of life, of a tranquil conscience born of virtuous living with Christ, of more and more abundant grace, of confidence in the Virgin without stain, and of overwhelming victory on a glad tomorrow.

As a child runs to its mother, when it is hurt or in fear, so we hasten to the Most Pure Heart of Mary when we are beset by temptation or doubt. She is as much interested in us or more than she was in the bride and bridegroom at Cana, equally prepared to speak the much-needed words of intercession on our behalf to Her Divine Son. As a result of her intercession, where sin abounded, "grace will more abound." Mary's love has not grown less nor the power of the Wonder Worker of Galilee been straitened. The Sacraments remain His fathomless channels of grace. May is a preparation for June. Mary will lead us to Jesus.

At times, perhaps, the Blessed Trinity may seem remote or even an abstract formula; not so our Heavenly Mother. We are her children on earth; we will still be her children in Paradise. We will find with her a safe refuge, a sure resting place, a most powerful Mediatrix with the Infinite Majesty of God.

The Holy Father, Pius XI, with his profound knowledge of the needs of his fellowmen, was well advised in designating for the month of May, five years ago, this important intention of confidence in the Most Pure Heart of Mary. In an age of insecurity and impurity he recommends confidence in the Tabernacle of the All-holy God. In an hour of unrest, agitation, and imminent revolution, he calls for cleanness of heart and the courage that is of God.

Seldom in history indeed has there been marked in men and women of all ages such a passion for security of tenure, permanence in employment, stabilized conditions of living, and assurance of a competence in the future. Every prophet who rises up in the land, ready to guarantee a fixed monthly income or a fresh distribution of wealth which will forever banish poverty and woe, is certain of a multitudinous following. Little is said of security of soul, of true inward happiness, of a system of values in which first things come first. And yet the economic chaos we behold is only a manifestation of a disorder of hearts and wills. The cure for selfishness and greed is to be sought in a restoration of God to His rightful place in modern society.

The present generation so largely without faith and bereft of a clear, unchanging code of conduct, is like a tree without roots. The branches will not put forth leaves, flowers and fruit until the tree has been once more rooted in the deep, rich soil of the Divine nature. Then it will flourish again with the life of supernatural grace.

Sin and insecurity go hand in hand. Untrue to his own better nature and uncertain of his fate on the morrow, the sinner naturally falls a prey to indecision, doubt, or even despair. The remedy is to escape the slavery of sin. But a saint is more than a deflated sinner. Sanctity means to put on Christ. And Christ is best found with His mother—at Bethlehem, at Nazareth, at Jerusalem, and in Heaven.

Security, we cannot repeat too often, is not primarily a matter of government or of economic reform or of social uplift, although all these have their place; it is fundamentally a matter of sinlessness and sacrifice. If Jesus and Mary tell us anything, they tell us that.

With that conviction we may go forth to labor in the morning and return home refreshed by the love we share with Mary for the Son of God, Her Son and our Brother. In a world of uncertainties we know no doubts. Approaching Jesus through Mary, we have the assurance only those can feel whose lives are an echo of the crowning beatitude: "Blessed are the pure of heart for they shall see God."

ADDENDA

The following historic item, concerning the author, was published in The New York Times, May 29, 1938.

DR. THORNING SETS RECORD
IN BUDAPEST BROADCAST
Wireless to The New York Times

BUDAPEST, Hungrary—By a record-breaking series of broadcasts to the United States, England, Ireland, Hungrary and other countries, an American priest, Dr. Joseph F. Thorning, of Mount St. Mary's College, Maryland, has become an outstanding figure at this year's Eucharistic Congress.

Never before in the history of broadcasting has an American priest enjoyed such a vast radio audience as has Dr. Thorning here. Besides three broadcasts to the United States over nation-wide hook-ups and a special program to Ireland and England, he also broadcast the congress proceedings in Hungarian, German, French and Spanish over other wave lengths.

The congress broadcasts have been carried over all the world by a score of radio companies.

181

MR. ICKES AND THE DARK AGES

Secretary's Reference to Medievalism Is Regarded
as Malapropos

To the Editor of The New York Times:

In our admiration for the scientific achievements of modern times we are hardly compelled to rehearse an erroneous version of medieval history. Least of all would we expect a distortion of historical truth at a meeting convoked to promote brotherly love as well as good-will. Consequently it is somewhat startling to read that Secretary of the Interior Harold L. Ickes, at a meeting of the Protestant Digest Associates "to combat racial and religious intolerance," drew a contrast between "the light of civilization" and "the darkness of the Middle Ages." Mr. Ickes' comparison, furthermore, was given in a context that suggested there was a parity between Hitlerism and medieval Christian culture.

The Secretary of the Interior has a sense of humor and he will appreciate the remark of a contemporaneous historian that "successive investigations keep pushing the 'Dark Ages' so much further and further back that they will probably ultimately cover no time whatever" (a quotation used by Dr. Lynn Thorndike, Professor of History in Columbia University, in his "Short History of Civilization," p. 295).

In the same chapter, among other illuminating disclosures, Dr. Thorndike submits a conclusion that is now quite generally accepted by historians. He writes (p. 299):

"We may therefore restrict the expression Dark Ages, which was once erroneously applied to the entire medieval period (i.e., c. 400-1500), merely to the early part of it. Even it is perhaps dark more in the sense that we lack information concerning much civilization during it than that we are sure it was an age of ignorance and backwardness. Indeed, it must be recognized that even the centuries from the fifth to the tenth contributed not a little to the formation of the civilization of the following period; only these seeds often did not come to harvest until later."

To be sure, some writers, with mistaken zeal, have tried to glorify the Middle Ages, stretching the evidence to cover

182

their extreme viewpoint. Fanatical interpretations, however, should scarcely keep us from maintaining the just, balanced opinion now widely shared by outstanding scholars.

Most people, I am sure, understand and condemn the horrors of Adolf Hitler's régime, in peace and in war. Secretary Ickes does not exaggerate on that score. At the same time, it would be comforting to have from this high official of our government equally frequent and equally devastating denunciations of Soviet totalitarianism. Now that Stalin and Hitler are partners in crime, evidence is daily increasing about the vicious character of the Communist domination of innocent populations. In these days of anxious tension, it is important to keep in focus the whole world picture.

Joseph F. Thorning,
Professor of Sociology and Social History,
Mount St. Mary's College

Emmitsburg, Md., Feb. 27, 1941.

(Published: March 4, 1941)